# CONFESSIONS

*of a* SERIAL

ENTERTAINER

# CONFESSIONS

## *of a* SERIAL

## ENTERTAINER

STEVEN STOLMAN

*Photographs by*

ALISSA DRAGUN

*Food Styling by Stacey Stolman*

**GIBBS SMITH**
TO ENRICH AND INSPIRE HUMANKIND

19 18 17 16 15          5 4 3 2 1

Published by
Gibbs Smith
P.O. Box 667
Layton, Utah 84041

1.800.835.4993 orders
www.gibbs-smith.com

Designed by Sheryl Dickert
Page production by Melissa Dymock
Food styling by Stacey Stolman
Printed and bound in Hong Kong

Gibbs Smith books are printed on either recycled, 100% post-consumer waste, FSC-certified papers or on paper produced from sustainable PEFC-certified forest/controlled wood source. Learn more at www.pefc.org.

Library of Congress Cataloging-in-Publication Data

Stolman, Steven.
  Confessions of a serial entertainer / Steven Stolman ; photographs by Alissa Dragun. — First edition.
     pages cm
  ISBN 978-1-4236-3715-8
1.  Entertaining. 2.  Cooking.  I. Title.
  TX731.S7368 2015
  642'.4—dc23
                    2014025642

◆◆◆

*To my late maternal grandparents, Sylvia and Jack Sloat,*

*my Nana and Poppy, who early on showed me the importance*

*of gracious hospitality in living a rich and fulfilling life.*

*At their table, there was always room for one more.*

# CONTENTS

# My Confession

◆◆◆

’m really not a very good cook. I don’t follow recipes and take all kinds of shortcuts.

I use a lot of stuff that comes out of bottles, jars, cans and boxes to create loose impressions of classical dishes that sometimes have absolutely no resemblance to the revered original. If you saw me in the kitchen, you’d be horrified. I’m not neat—and I have a tendency to do something, screw it up and do it over. I have no knife skills. I burn things—or undercook them. I serve hot foods cold and cold foods lukewarm. My sauces curdle, and I have been known to save things with a slurry of cornstarch and water. I overdress salads and use way too many utensils. When no one is looking, I will throw in a slurp of Gravy Master, as I don’t have the patience to let things brown on their own. I have never made a proper stock. Yet I am known as a rather accomplished host and, more ironically, a chef.

Now don’t get me wrong; I do love to cook. There is ample discussion in this book regarding my psychological need to entertain. And while I actually did take a class with Julia Child (something that I won in a recipe contest), most of what I know about cooking comes from public television and sitting at the counter at luncheonettes.

I love nothing more than watching a short order cook wield a spatula on a flattop. Many times, in front of my own stove, I fantasize about having an expanse of greased stainless steel before me and creating heaping plates of wonderfulness. I hear the clatter of those heavy Buffalo china dishes and the chatter of wisecracking waitresses. At least I can crack an egg with one hand and flip things in a skillet, and, courtesy of Julia Child, I can make a perfect omelet roll up on itself and deposit it onto the plate with the flick of my wrist. But it ends there.

So why on earth would I even think about writing a cookbook? Well, obviously because I can, but, in actuality, I feel like I have a story to tell and experiences to share. Just to look at me, it's clear that I enjoy food. But I also enjoy talking about it and reading about it. My collection of vintage cookbooks, especially those put out by ladies' charity groups or time-honored restaurants, continues to grow. Every Labor Day weekend in Fish Creek, Wisconsin, the local library does a book sale in a big white tent near the boat docks: "$1 each," proclaim the signs next to piles of dog-eared paperbacks and old travel books. And while most people leave the tent with things like James Patterson's latest and greatest, I trill with delight over the likes of *Favorite Congealed Salads of Episcopal Women.*

It's late nights pouring over these spiral-bound compilations that seems to give me extraordinary comfort. The ladies who submitted these recipes cooked like I do, with ingredients like mayonnaise and Worcestershire sauce and the kind of packaged stuff one would expect to find in the pantry of a fallout shelter. So these are the recipes that I most enjoy sharing—the kind of concoctions that would make today's typical foodie cringe but are the first to disappear when they make an appearance on my table.

I'm also sharing the recipes of relatives and friends, not so much for the tastes—although many of these dishes are indeed delicious—but for specific food memories. While my Aunt Trina's chicken is a crowd pleaser, I honestly don't think I ever had it cooked by my Aunt Trina. It was my mom who made it often, in a big blue Dansk Kobenstyle pan. It was the ultimate do-ahead dish, and I remember seeing it often in our West Hartford kitchen, defrosting atop an indoor gas grill that we never turned on because it made such a mess. But that big pan of sautéed chicken breasts, with their eggy coating and fragrant topping of mushrooms and dry vermouth, meant so much more than something good to eat. It meant that company was coming, and that always made me very happy. It still does.

# A Disclaimer

◆◆◆

There are recipes in this book that many readers will recognize. Some are part of our popular culture, such as California Onion Dip, which is probably the first thing one learns to make beyond toast. Others make frequent appearances in the hundreds of spiral-bound charity cookbooks that are part of my prized collection. Regardless of what one calls the combination of Pillsbury crescent rolls and some kind of brown sugar and butter goo, it's basically all the same stuff.

Of course I don't claim to have created any of these. In some cases, I have added my own little twists, but in others, there was simply no way to improve upon the original. I have seen recipes that encourage people to make their own homemade cream of chicken soup to add to recipes calling for cream of chicken soup, but to me, this borders on insanity. I have made my own mayonnaise and totally understand why it's better, or at least better for you. But there is a very certain flavor sensation that can only be had with Duke's or Hellmann's. I suppose much of this has to do with flavor memory, and our minds can certainly play tricks on us.

My little niece dotes on Kraft Macaroni and Cheese. For her, it's a safe haven in the world of suspicious foods that seven-year-olds inhabit. She gobbles it up with gusto at her own home, where it is prepared by a mother whom she trusts and served on a plate that she recognizes with a fork that she likes. But—wouldn't you know it?—when I make it for her, following the directions on the box to the letter, using the same milk and butter that her mother buys, she refuses to eat it, saying it's "different." I swear, I don't sneak in a pinch of cayenne pepper or nutmeg or a few shreds of Gruyère like I want to. *It's exactly the same as her mother makes it.* But to my niece's discerning palate, it's Lobster Thermidor, a dish she would no sooner touch than pickled rattlesnake.

We call certain dishes comfort foods because they take us back to simpler, happier times. Tuna noodle casserole, especially in a Corningware baking dish, will always transport me back to our family kitchen on Brookside Boulevard, with its '70s mod indoor-outdoor carpeting and royal blue Naugahyde dinette set. At once, I'm twelve years old and fat and miserable, but the feeling is still warm and fuzzy.

There are recipes in this book that are just plain silly—like cutting a hole in a piece of bread and frying an egg in it. But napped with a little ketchup and maybe a sprinkle of grated Parmesan cheese, it's nothing short of wonderful. And there are dishes that I have enjoyed in great restaurants and have tried to simplify for home cooks like me, who lack backyard herb gardens and sous-vide machines. I have had the amazing bouillabaisse in St. Tropez at that charming place known for it back in the day. My version is so much simpler and floats my boat. The same with my paella, which any Barcelonan worth his lisp would probably laugh at. My cassoulet, or what I cavalierly call cassoulet, has no duck confit or goose fat. It's basically just beans and chicken, but in the kitchen of my mind, it's lusty and luscious. After a few bottles of wine, even my most sophisticated friends agree that it's pretty damn good cassoulet.

I hope that this book gives you as much pleasure reading it as it has given me to write it. I have never looked at cooking or entertaining as a chore, but this sure has been a labor of love.

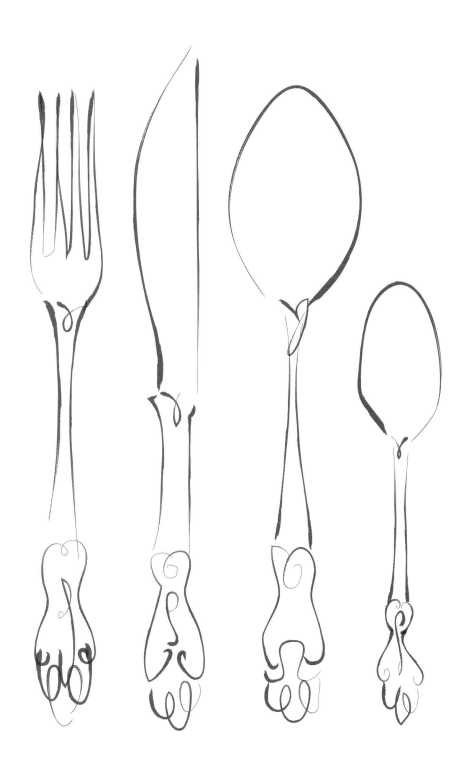

# EVERYTHING HAPPENS
# AT COCKTAILS

◆◆◆

At the risk of sounding boastful, my other half, Rich, and I throw one helluva cocktail party. And while it sounds glamorous to say that we have three homes, the reality is that they are all quite modest—even tiny. In our house in the Milwaukee suburbs, a 1950s ranch built into a hillside, we think nothing of inviting the entire neighborhood over for drinks. In the small 1960s studio apartment we live in on New York's Upper East Side, if Michigan is playing (football, basketball, you name it), we're usually hosting, as we have fellow Michigan alums as neighbors, and it just grows exponentially from there. And in our 1970s one-bedroom Palm Beach condo, *that*'s where we really love to pack 'em in.

Over the years, a formula has emerged that works. Once or twice a season (it sounds grand, but what I mean is the period from late fall to late spring, when Palm Beach is at peak occupancy), we'll host what is lovingly called a "town sweep." The guest list includes everybody who has ever invited us to anything, along with assorted family and friends to round it out. Without trying, we typically end up with 90 to 100 guests. This remains an enormous source of pride, because in Palm Beach weekend events are stacked up like incoming flights at O'Hare. We're told that folks love to come to our parties because of the eclectic mix of people (think the opening party scene of *Auntie Mame*) and, surprisingly, the food.

"Sweetie, it isn't about the food!" I was lectured by the sharp-witted fashion editor of the local paper. Yet that seems to be what people remember. We hire a handsome, able-bodied bartender who brings with him several boxes of all-purpose wine glasses and a big chest of ice. We station him at the wet bar in our entrance hall so that incoming guests get a drink right off the bat, and we put out a spread on the round table in the dining area. If it's a special occasion, like a party thrown in someone's honor (my favorite), we'll hire an additional waiter or two to pass hors d'oeuvre. (Does that sound funny to you— *hors d'oeuvre* instead of *hors d'oeuvres*? Well, one of my mentor hostesses, a brilliantly stylish public school teacher, taught me the correct usage. In French, the *hors* is plural, not the *oeuvre*. So there.)

If it's early in the season, we'll call the party from 6:30–8:30 p.m., as it gets dark early and, hopefully, we can throw open the sliding glass doors and allow the party to spill out onto the apartment's rather large terrace. But if we do this anytime after the 1st of April, the setting sun blasts into the living room with such intensity that we have to keep the curtains drawn. At this time of year, we start and end things a bit later, more like 7:30–9:30 p.m.

"Why only two hours?" you may ask. My philosophy is that anything longer gets sloppy. It's cocktails, not dinner, and Palm Beachers are used to this convention, as are New Yorkers, where people like to stop by for a drink and then move on to dinner at a restaurant or someone else's home.

This is *not* true in Milwaukee, and I learned that the hard way. In the Midwest, people

like to stay and stay. Our first neighborhood cocktail party, planned the same way as our Palm Beach parties, turned into a five-hour bacchanal. After two hours, all the food was gone, but the people weren't. Next time, I will call it for seven o'clock and have a simple buffet prepared plus an emergency supply of frozen pizzas in the freezer.

But back to our wonderful Palm Beach cocktail parties: I always take my cues from far more experienced hosts than I.

The most memorable parties are the simplest ones, with fresh, homemade, tasty food that isn't hard to figure out or eat. My crowd-pleaser menus always feature pigs in blankets with good horseradish mustard, served in abundance on either silver trays or beautiful platters. Then I like to offer little cocktail sandwiches—tea sandwiches, really—a mix of smoked salmon, homemade chicken salad or sliced cucumber with cream cheese. While at first glance these may seem old-fashioned or even fuddy-duddy, I love them for their liquor absorption. Besides, I think they are charming, as long as they are absolutely perfect and look as though they were cut by a laser beam.

On the dining table, I like to set up at least one glamorous silver chafing dish with Swedish meatballs or a baked dip, as it really sets the tone. I also put out one of my funny retro cocktail spreads: egg salad with bacon, cheddar cheese with bacon—actually, anything with bacon—or something involving olives and cream cheese. In a world of satays, cones and lollipops, my cocktail menu items may seem a bit pastiche, but it's my party, and I'll serve what I want to.

## Don't Be Shy

The joke among our friends is that while Rich and I live in the smallest of places, we entertain the most out of anybody. And while much of this is due to my own shtick of needing to have people around me all of the time and being a control freak and just about any other psychotic label you want to slap on my forehead, the truth of the matter is that I'd rather have people in than go out. This really isn't a problem, because, with a few exceptions, nobody else ever seems to invite us over.

In New York, especially, there seems to be this fear factor that keeps people from opening their homes. Frankly, I find meeting at bars or restaurants kind of sad, so without fail I will always badger friends to begin the evening with at least a drink and a potato chip at our place. And people seem genuinely pleased to come over, as they know our bar is always stocked and there will always be something good to nibble on.

But there are those who never—and I mean NEVER—have anyone in, so this chapter is dedicated to you. I don't care if you live in a penthouse or a fifth-floor walk-up; for crying out loud, buy a bottle of wine and a can of peanuts and call me!

I think that much of the dread to entertain comes from an inability to be spontaneous, from thinking that one's home isn't up to snuff and, simply, from not having the basics on hand to have people in at a moment's notice. Buying a box of six inexpensive wine glasses at Pier One is a step in the right direction. Buying two or three boxes is even better.

And just as one keeps a mental shopping list of staples for trips to the supermarket, you know, toilet paper, yogurt, Dijon mustard—which totally blows me away because if you never cook, why do you need Dijon mustard?—but maybe, just maybe add to this list a pack of white cocktail napkins and a box of Triscuits. Trust me: seeing these things in your kitchen cupboard will give you the strength for a breakthrough.

For those willing to heed my call and take the plunge, here are a few foolproof little cocktail snacks that involve very few ingredients or preparation time but deliver big flavor and will keep them coming back for more, which may or may not be what you really want.

# MATER'S MESS

*Serves 6 to 8*

1 cup pimento-stuffed olives

1 yellow onion, coarsely chopped

8 ounces cream cheese, softened

2 hard-boiled eggs, peeled

1 cup shredded cheddar cheese

Crackers or cucumber slices, for serving

Place olives, onion, cream cheese, eggs, and shredded cheese in a food processor fitted with a steel blade; pulse until well combined. Transfer to a serving bowl, cover, and refrigerate until ready to serve.

Serve with crackers or cucumber slices.

# THAT OLD ARTICHOKE DIP

*Serves 6 to 8. Multiply for larger groups.*

1 (14-ounce) can quartered artichoke hearts

2 tablespoons minced onion

$1/4$ cup mayonnaise

$1/4$ cup sour cream

$1/3$ cup grated Parmesan cheese

$1/4$ cup sliced almonds

Preheat the oven to 375°F.

Drain artichokes and chop coarsely. In a medium bowl, combine artichokes, onion, mayonnaise, sour cream, and Parmesan cheese. Pour mixture into a 2-cup ovenproof baking dish. Top with almonds and bake for 20 minutes, or until golden and bubbly.

# DR. NAGY'S PÂTÉ

*Serves 10 to 12*

¼ cup water, boiling

1 envelope unflavored gelatin

2 tablespoons butter

1 medium shallot, minced

1 pint chicken livers, drained and rinsed

1 tablespoon chili powder

1 teaspoon salt

½ teaspoon cracked black pepper

½ cup dry sherry

8 ounces cream cheese

Sliced lemons, for garnish

Crackers or Melba rounds, for serving

Pour the boiling water into a small bowl and stir in the gelatin. Set aside.

In a large sauté pan, melt butter on medium-high heat until foaming subsides. Add the shallot and cook for 3 to 4 minutes, until golden.

Add livers, chili powder, salt, and pepper. Cook until the livers are firm and no longer pink. Deglaze the pan with sherry, and continue cooking until sherry has evaporated.

Transfer mixture to a food processor fitted with a steel blade. Add cream cheese and gelatin, and pulse until smooth. Transfer to a terrine, cover, and refrigerate overnight, or until firm. Garnish pâté with lemon slices.

Serve with crackers or Melba rounds.

# HAPPY NANCY

*Serves 6 to 8*

8 ounces cream cheese, room temperature

1 jar pepper jelly

Carr's Table Water Crackers

Place cream cheese on your prettiest serving plate, top with jelly, and serve with crackers.

# PIMENTO CHEESE

*Serves 6 to 8*

2 cups shredded cheddar cheese

1 (4-ounce) jar diced pimentos, drained

$1/2$ cup mayonnaise

$1/2$ teaspoon cayenne pepper

Salt

Ritz crackers or celery sticks, to serve

Place cheese, pimentos, mayonnaise, and pepper in the bowl of a food processor fitted with a steel blade; pulse until well combined. Season the mixture with salt to taste. Transfer to a serving bowl, cover, and refrigerate until ready to serve.

Serve with Ritz crackers, celery sticks, or anything your heart desires.

# GRECO CALIFORNIA DIP

*Serves 6 to 8*

1 pint 2% plain Greek yogurt

1 packet onion soup mix

Sweet potato chips

Combine yogurt and soup mix. Chill for at least 1 hour for flavor to develop and for dried onions to soften. Transfer to a bowl and serve with a generous quantity of sweet potato chips.

# CURRY DIP

*Serves 6 to 8*

1 cup 2% plain Greek yogurt

1 cup mayonnaise

1 tablespoon curry powder

Salt and freshly ground black pepper

An abundant array of washed and trimmed raw
vegetables, such as jicama, zucchini, celery,
radishes, carrots, or bell pepper, all cut into strips,
sticks, or rounds—whatever you like for dipping

Whisk together the yogurt, mayonnaise, and curry powder. Season
with salt and pepper to taste. Chill before serving.

Serve in a pretty bowl with the vegetables presented in a wicker
basket or on a ceramic platter.

# Dip Do's and Don'ts

It's no secret that I have a thing for 1950s cocktail dips and spreads, the kind of things that invariably involve some kind of shredded cheese and a savory modifier, like olives or bacon. This obsession probably comes from my childhood, when Kraft Olive Pimento Spread (since discontinued) was a regular habituate of our kitchen cabinet. Nothing tasted better than this unnaturally pink stuff, especially when licked from a finger. And the empty jars were cleverly designed to be washed out and reused as juice glasses. How chic!

Of course, the real reason for my love of cocktail spreads is for all of the little gadgets required to serve them properly. What would cocktail spreads be without little spreaders, especially ones with handles fashioned to look like fruits and vegetables? Or embellished ones, with little shells or beads, perhaps faux tortoise shell or shagreen? I have to admit, I love them all.

I also love cheese boards, marbles and footed glass serving pieces, although I detest chip 'n' dip bowls. We did have a fabulous Dansk teak thing that spun on ball bearings like a lazy Susan and had compartments with removable glass dishes. That I wish I still had!

The southern staple pimento cheese probably tops my list of favorite spreads. There is no comparison between homemade and store bought, and I cannot think of an easier recipe: cheese, mayonnaise, pimentos and cayenne pepper, basta! Its success is really about the grind of the cheese (fine shreds), the kind of mayonnaise (only Duke's will do) and the amount of time allowed for the flavors to bloom in the fridge and get really cold. This aspect is key for any spread or dip, especially those that involve dry ingredients like onion soup mix mixed with things like sour cream or cream cheese.

My second favorite spread would be the enigmatic Jane's Cheese. I love any dish that defies description, and it always amuses me to hear people guess what's in it. I mean, you just gotta love a dish that everyone swears is chicken salad yet has absolutely nothing to do with chicken!

EVERYTHING HAPPENS AT COCKTAILS

# JANE'S CHEESE

*Serves 6 to 8*

1 bunch scallions

1 (4.3-ounce) package crumbled cooked bacon

4 cups shredded cheddar cheese

½ cup mayonnaise

Dash of Worcestershire sauce

Freshly ground black pepper

Crackers, for serving

Combine scallions, bacon, cheese, mayonnaise, and Worcestershire sauce in a food processor fitted with a steel blade. Pulse mixture until combined. Transfer to a serving bowl and season with pepper to taste. Chill before serving.

Serve with very simple crackers.

# TARRAGON MUSTARD SAUCE

*Makes about 1 cup*

1 cup mayonnaise

1 tablespoon Dijon mustard

1 teaspoon dried tarragon

Precooked shrimp, for serving

In a medium bowl, combine all ingredients, cover, and refrigerate overnight.

Serve with ice-cold shrimp.

# ASPARAGUS ROULADES

*Serves 6 to 8*

12 slices Pepperidge Farms white sandwich bread

8 ounces cream cheese, softened

1 (10-ounce) can asparagus spears, drained

1 cup (2 sticks) butter, melted

Remove crusts from bread and discard. Flatten bread with a rolling pin. On each slice of bread, spread cream cheese and place an asparagus spear; then roll up jelly-roll style.

Place in freezer and freeze until hard.

Preheat the oven to 450°F.

Remove the roulades from the freezer, cut in half, and dip the entire piece in melted butter. Place on a sheet pan lined with parchment paper and bake for 8 to 10 minutes, until golden brown and crispy.

# CHEESY POUFS

*Serves 6 to 8*

1 pound Jimmy Dean's sausage roll

2 cups Bisquick

2⅓ cups shredded cheddar cheese

½ cup water

1 teaspoon coarse ground black pepper

Preheat the oven to 350°F. Grease an 18 x 13-inch baking sheet and set aside.

Combine all ingredients in a large bowl. Mix well and shape into 1-inch balls. Place balls 1 inch apart on baking sheet. Bake for 20 to 25 minutes, until golden brown.

Cheesy poufs may be frozen after baking. To reheat, arrange on baking sheet and cover with aluminum foil. Warm at 350°F for 20 minutes.

# EGG SALAD WITH BACON

*Serves 6 to 8*

1 dozen large hard-boiled eggs, peeled

1 cup mayonnaise

1 teaspoon dry mustard

1/2 teaspoon salt

1/2 teaspoon coarse black pepper

2 (4.3-ounce) packages crumbled bacon

Ritz crackers or Melba rounds, for serving

Run eggs through an egg slicer twice to chop. Or use a method of your choice. Place eggs in a large bowl and mix with mayonnaise, mustard, salt, and pepper. Transfer to a serving bowl, cover, and chill. Sprinkle bacon on top just before serving.

Serve with Ritz crackers or Melba rounds.

## *What to wear to a cocktail party?*

Even though I have spent a great deal of my career as a fashion designer and retailer, doling out advice, nothing amuses me more than the question "What should I wear?" It makes me want to answer, "Clothes." I mean, if one has gotten through life to the point of being adequately evolved enough to be invited to cocktail parties, one ought to know how to dress.

Don't get me wrong; I do enjoy seeing someone beautifully turned out, for any occasion, as long as it isn't overwrought or self-consciously stylish. Sigourney Weaver had a great line in *Working Girl* that was supposedly attributed to Coco Chanel; but even if it wasn't, it's so true: "Dress shabbily, they notice the dress. Dress impeccably, they notice the woman." And the same goes for a man.

A legendary Palm Beach hostess once gave me this interesting guide:

Formal: Tuxedos for men and gowns or cocktail dresses for women, with jewelry.

Informal: Suits or sport coats and ties for men, cocktail dresses for women, with jewelry.

Casual: Sport coats and open shirts for men, cocktail pajamas for women, with jewelry.

Very casual: Open shirts for men, shirts and simple pants for women, and maybe just a jeweled sandal.

Jeez! And yet there is another couple in Palm Beach who invariably shows up looking like they just washed up on shore—with sandy arms and legs and seaweed in their hair—no matter what the occasion or the weather. I get it. You like the beach. Go home and change, or at least shower.

For the few who haven't mastered dressing yet, or simply like to be told what to do, I offer the following suggestions:

Don't be afraid to overdress. No one will ever look down upon you for looking *better* than everyone else. I'm not suggesting black tie for a picnic, but looking like one has taken some care in putting together an outfit is, as Martha Stewart says, a very good thing. In a private home in a casual setting, jeans and a great shirt or sweater and nice shoes are perfect. If a guy wants to add a tie and a sport coat, terrific. If a woman wants to wear a dress and heels, why not?

Women, really think through the purse situation. If you are at a stand-up cocktail party with a drink in one hand and an hors d'oeuvre in the other, how are you going to juggle a gigantic handbag without looking like a goof-ball? Consider a little shoulder bag or a clutch that tucks under the arm. Or better yet, a dress with pockets. And then there's that little ritual of women wanting to hide their purse somewhere: "I'll just put it behind this chair (and totally screw up your furniture plan)."

Don't wear clothes that take up a lot of room. The fun of a cocktail party is the crush. Leave dresses with hoop skirts and petticoats for other occasions.

Think about how you look from the waist up, as that's how people see you at a stand-up cocktail party. Men, think about a natty blazer and a crisp white shirt and a pocket square. Women, consider a beautiful tailored shirt and a dramatic necklace. White shirts highlight one's smile and eyes. There's a reason why they are so popular. There is no excuse for not owning a good white shirt. See: Carolina Herrera.

A little sparkle isn't a bad thing for a cocktail party. I think it's festive and fun. These days, though, it seems like everything has sequins and beads, from T-shirts to socks. Be judicious and try for glamour rather than bedazzled.

Don't sweat it. Literally. If you get hot in a crowded room, wear cool clothing. There's nothing less riveting than hearing someone whine, "It's so hot in here!" You know what they say: If you can't stand the heat . . .

Communicate through your dress that you appreciate being invited. Make an effort. Nonchalance is one thing; ambivalence is just plain insulting.

# HEALTHIER SWEDISH MEATBALLS

*Serves 6 to 8*

2 tablespoons cornstarch

$\frac{1}{2}$ cup water

1 package (24–28 count) prepared
frozen turkey meatballs

1 ($10\frac{3}{4}$-ounce) can double strength beef broth

1 cup 2% plain Greek yogurt

1 tablespoon Worcestershire sauce

1 teaspoon thyme

Salt and freshly ground black pepper

In a small bowl, dissolve cornstarch in water; set aside.

In a large skillet, heat meatballs and broth. Stir in yogurt, Worcestershire, and thyme. Bring to a boil and whisk in cornstarch mixture. Season with salt and pepper to taste.

Serve in a silver chafing dish with toothpicks.

# THAT '70S QUICHE

*Serves 6 to 8*

1 tablespoon butter

½ cup chopped onion

1 egg

1 cup milk

1½ cups Bisquick

1 cup grated cheddar cheese, divided

3 tablespoons butter, melted

2 teaspoons poppy seeds

Preheat the oven to 400°F. Grease a 9-inch pie pan and set aside.

In a medium sauté pan, melt butter over medium-high heat and cook onion until soft and translucent. Set aside.

In a large bowl, whisk together egg and milk. Add Bisquick, onions, and ½ cup cheese. Pour into pie pan, brush with melted butter, and sprinkle with remaining ½ cup cheese and poppy seeds. Bake for 20 minutes.

Serve warm.

# SALMON MOUSSE

*Serves 10 to 12*

1 envelope unflavored gelatin

$\frac{1}{2}$ cup water, divided

1 ($10\frac{3}{4}$-ounce) can condensed tomato soup

8 ounces cream cheese, softened

1 cup mayonnaise

1 can salmon, bones and skin removed (or buy boneless poached salmon)

$\frac{1}{4}$ cup minced Vidalia onion

1 cup coarsely chopped celery

1 loaf cocktail pumpernickel bread, plain crackers, or cucumber slices, for serving

Dissolve gelatin in $\frac{1}{4}$ cup of water and set aside.

In a small saucepan over medium heat, heat soup with remaining $\frac{1}{4}$ cup water. When soup is heated through, add gelatin, remove from heat, and allow to cool.

In a food processor fitted with a metal blade, combine cream cheese, tomato mixture, mayonnaise, salmon, and onion; pulse until smooth. Remove blade and fold in celery.

Grease a fish-shaped mold with vegetable oil and pour mixture into mold. Cover and refrigerate overnight.

When it is time to remove the mousse from the mold, place the mold in a bowl filled with warm water for just a few seconds; be careful not

to let water get into the
mousse. Place a platter
on top of the mold and
invert quickly to release
the mousse.

Serve with either cocktail
pumpernickel bread,
plain crackers, or on
cucumber slices.

# STAND-UP DEVILED EGGS

### *Makes 24*

1 dozen hard-boiled eggs, peeled

²/₃ cup mayonnaise

2 teaspoons mustard powder

Paprika or chopped parsley

Cut the eggs in half widthwise. Remove the yolks and transfer to a medium bowl. Gently slice a sliver off the bottom of each white half so that they stand up.

Mix together egg yolks, mayonnaise, and mustard. Place mixture in a pastry bag fitted with a star tip, or use a ziplock bag and snip off the corner. Pipe yolk mixture into the whites and sprinkle with paprika or chopped parsley.

# SEAFOOD NEWBURG

*Serves 6 to 8*

¼ cup butter

¼ cup flour

2 cups half & half

1 tablespoon sweet paprika

2 tablespoons Worcestershire sauce

1 cup dry sherry

1 pound peeled and deveined raw shrimp

1 pound bay scallops

Puff pastry shells, at least one per person

In a medium pot, melt butter over high heat until bubbling subsides. Reduce heat to medium and add flour; cook for 2 to 3 minutes. Whisk in half & half; continue whisking to remove lumps. Reduce heat and simmer for 5 to 8 minutes. Stir in paprika, Worcestershire, and sherry. Simmer slowly for 5 minutes. Add seafood and cook for no more than 2 to 3 minutes, being very careful not to overcook seafood.

Arrange pastry shells in a deep silver bowl and let guests serve themselves. Keep seafood mixture warm in a chafing dish if you are not serving immediately.

# TEA SANDWICHES

*Serves 12 to 24 people*

6 loaves potato bread, preferably
half white and half wheat

1 (4-pound) container of prepared chicken salad

2 pounds sliced smoked salmon

4 seedless cucumbers, peeled,
sliced, salted, and drained*

Mayonnaise

The key to making perfect tea sandwiches is organization and lots of room to work. And the secret weapon: an electric carving knife. If you don't have one, get one. It makes all the difference.

Every slice of bread needs to be lightly covered with mayonnaise, except those being used in conjunction with filling already containing mayonnaise.

*\* Drain for at least 30 minutes to draw off as much liquid as possible.*

*continued>*

On a large, clean work surface, lay the bread out in the order it comes off the loaf. Spread a very thin coating of mayonnaise on all slices, except those receiving chicken salad. The mayonnaise acts as a moisture barrier and prevents soggy sandwiches.

Arrange smoked salmon, cucumber slices, and chicken salad in a single, even layer on alternating rows of bread leaving corresponding rows unfilled. Make sure fillings are applied smoothly and evenly. Do not be concerned about laying fillings all the way out to the edges of the bread slices, as these will be trimmed off in the cutting process.

Cover every filled slice with a corresponding unfilled slice. Stack in piles of 2 complete sandwiches. Using an electric carving knife, trim off all the crusts. Continuing with the electric carving knife, cut sandwiches into quarters. Store sandwiches in an aluminum foil container with sheets of damp paper towel placed between the layers. Seal entire pan completely with plastic wrap and place in the refrigerator until ready to serve.

# The Party's Over

As much as I love to entertain, I also love to sleep. Well, not really sleep, as I am practically an insomniac, but I do love to put on an old college sweatshirt and tartan boxer shorts and crawl under the covers to read my iPad or watch "House Hunters" until my eyelids get heavy. Sadly, this usually wants to happen about an hour before my guests are ready to leave. So what's a host to do?

This is why I love cocktail parties, as they generally happen at the beginning of an evening. Everyone is fresh and amusing instead of sloppy and wind bagged. But for as many of us who like to start early and be in dreamland before the late news comes on, there are just as many who love to go on and on. Don't get me wrong, I've had my share of "one more drink and let's solve the world's problems" kind of nights. But honestly, once I owned my own business and was responsible for opening one of my stores in the morning, I lost interest in those long night's journeys into days.

My other half likes to stay up later than I do and requires far less sleep. This has proven helpful in our entertaining as I can simply do a "French Goodbye" and trundle off to bed while he keeps the party going. He also cleans the kitchen before he comes to bed, so you will never hear me complain. I do feel badly for folks who don't have this kind of strategic partner. There's always the protracted yawns or the frequent looking at one's watch that usually does the trick in getting people to mosey. But if all else fails, get out the vacuum or close down the bar or both. After that, you're on your own. Sorry.

# CHICKEN HASH FOR A CROWD

*Serves 10 to 12. Multiply for larger crowds.*

8 ounces chopped bacon

4–5 boneless, skinless chicken breasts

2 cups water

2 cups dry vermouth

2 bay leaves

1 tablespoon salt, divided, plus more

1 tablespoon freshly ground black pepper, plus more

½ cup (1 stick) butter

1 cup flour

4 cups half & half

4 cups dry sherry

1 tablespoon ground nutmeg

Pinch of cayenne pepper

Cooked brown and wild rice

This is a cocktail buffet staple, when passed hors d'oeuvre just aren't enough.

In a medium pan, cook bacon until crisp. Drain on paper towels and set aside.

In a large sauté pan, add chicken, water, vermouth, and bay leaves; season with salt and pepper. To poach the chicken, bring the liquid to a boil over high heat, then reduce heat to a simmer and cover;

simmer until chicken is cooked through. Remove pan from heat and allow chicken to cool in the cooking liquid.

Shred the chicken by hand into small pieces.

In a medium pot, melt butter over medium-high heat until the foaming subsides. Whisk in flour and cook for 2 to 3 minutes. Slowly whisk in half & half and sherry, making sure to break up the lumps. Stir in nutmeg, a big pinch of salt and pepper and cayenne. Simmer for 10 minutes. Stir in chicken and transfer mixture to a chafing dish.

Sprinkle with bacon.

Serve on small plates accompanied by a mixture of brown and wild rice.

# DINNER FOR THE BOSS

This was the title of one of Julia Child's iconic episodes from *Julia Child and Company*, the late '70s series that truly influenced how I still cook today. Julia was at her best—informative, engaging, and *very* funny. The set was light and bright and the recipes that she presented were totally accessible. To this day, nothing relaxes me more than a private little Julia Child marathon on YouTube. I suppose it's because I am taken back to a rather carefree time. The "Dinner for the Boss" episode featured a standing rib roast, which will always have a soft spot in my heart. It's certainly not for everyday. But as a once-in-a-great-while treat, this king of the butcher counter can't be beat.

A standing rib roast was always my mom's go-to for important dinners. It's such a retro dish and not at all in keeping with the shift towards lighter fare, but it is a menu item that every good cook should have tucked away in his or her repertoire. I've included a method that I have found to be foolproof for this extravagant cut of meat.

I am including the other dishes that my mom traditionally served along with prime rib, plus a few of my own.

## The Importance of Silver

In this age of super-casual living, where plates are square and tables are high, the idea of gleaming silver seems terribly old fashioned. But, to me, there is nothing more beautiful. Early on, I scrounged thrift shops and yard sales for silver serving pieces that others felt dated or worse, didn't want.

I know, I know—silver is a pain to polish. In places like Palm Beach, it seems to tarnish immediately, from either the humidity or lack of constant use. But I am immensely proud of my collection of Revere bowls, wine coasters, serving trays, candlesticks and chafing dishes. I have a set of coin silver spoons that has been added to over decades and a pair of scalloped oval bowls that catch the candlelight in the most alluring ways.

I grew up in a family that truly cherished silver. Full sets of sterling silver flatware were considered de rigueur for civilized dining. And since we kept kosher, there was one set of Georg Jensen for meat meals and one for dairy. The meat set, the iconic Acorn pattern, was a wedding gift to my parents from my great-grandmother in 1954. The dairy set was purchased by my grandparents on a trip to Denmark. My Nana packed it in her luggage; I have no clue if she declared it. But she did put one knife in her purse in the event that it was lost or impounded, just to show my mother what she *would* have gotten.

When I finally found someone crazy enough to marry me, my parents gave us their Acorn set as a wedding gift. To be able to set as lovely and gracious a table as my parents do and grandparents did is one of the great pleasures of my life, even if it does mean finding myself up to my elbows in Hagerty Silver Foam. For cocktail parties, I haul out every possible piece of silver and plan menus around it. To me, it sets a tone—a bit retro, but in this era of self-consciously stylish tablescapes, oddly charming. At least that's what my friends tell me. Maybe they're just being nice.

# WALLIS SIMPSON'S POPOVERS

*Makes 6*

3 tablespoons melted butter

2 eggs

1 cup milk, warmed

1 cup all-purpose flour

$\frac{1}{2}$ teaspoon kosher salt

Preheat the oven to 450°F. Pour 1 teaspoon of melted butter into each of the 6 cups in a popover tin and set aside. You can use ordinary muffin tins, but leave every other well empty to allow for a nice big popover.

In a blender, combine all the ingredients and blend until smooth. Pour the batter into the popover tins until $\frac{2}{3}$ full and bake for 20 minutes, during which time the popovers will puff. Reduce heat to 375°F and continue baking for an additional 20 minutes, or until golden and crisp.

# MOCK MULLIGATAWNY

*Serves 6 to 8*

4 tablespoons butter

1 medium onion, chopped

1 tablespoon curry powder

4 tablespoons all-purpose flour

1 quart low-sodium chicken broth

2 cups half & half

$^1/_2$ teaspoon cayenne pepper

Salt

Plain Greek yogurt, for garnish

Chopped peanuts, for garnish

Chopped parsley, for garnish

In a medium soup pot, melt butter over medium-high heat until the foaming subsides, then sauté the onion until soft. Add curry powder and continue cooking for 1 to 2 minutes to release the aroma. Dust mixture with flour and cook for 2 to 3 minutes, stirring constantly. Pour in the chicken broth and whisk vigorously, making sure there are no lumps. Allow mixture to thicken. Add half & half and season with cayenne and salt to taste.

Serve soup with a dollop of yogurt and garnish with peanuts and parsley.

# A RIFF ON CAESAR SALAD

*Serves 6*

Romaine lettuce, torn bite-size

1 pint cherry tomatoes*

Blender Caesar Dressing (recipe below)

Toss lettuce and tomatoes with Blender Caesar Dressing. Divide among serving plates.

*My mom always added these. Don't ask why.*

## BLENDER CAESAR DRESSING

$2/3$ cup olive oil

$1/3$ cup red wine vinegar

1 tin flat fillet anchovies

2 cloves garlic

1 tablespoon Dijon mustard

2 tablespoons Parmesan cheese

Place ingredients in a blender and blend until smooth and creamy.

# NICKY AMY'S ASPARAGUS

*Serves 4*

1 pound asparagus, cleaned

¼ cup extra virgin olive oil

Juice of 1 lemon

Coarse salt

Freshly ground black pepper

Steam asparagus for 3 to 5 minutes, until bright green and crisp-tender. Remove from pan immediately and plunge into a bowl of water and ice and set aside.

Whisk together olive oil and lemon juice.

Drizzle dressing over asparagus and sprinkle with coarse salt and pepper.

# SIMPLY SAUTÉED CHERRY TOMATOES

*Serves 4 to 6*

2 tablespoons olive oil

2 pints ripe cherry tomatoes

$\frac{1}{2}$ cup basil leaves, cut into thin strips

Kosher salt and coarse ground black pepper

Heat oil in a large sauté pan over medium-high heat. Add cherry tomatoes and sauté for 5 to 8 minutes, until soft and skins begin to wrinkle. Stir in basil and season with salt and pepper to taste.

# TRISH'S CHICKEN FLORENTINE

*Serves 4*

1 pound boneless, skinless chicken breasts

2 teaspoons kosher salt, divided

1 teaspoon coarse ground black pepper, divided

2 tablespoons all-purpose flour

2 tablespoons extra virgin olive oil

1 ($10^3/_4$-ounce) can cream of chicken soup

1 cup mayonnaise

Juice of 1 lemon

1 (16-ounce) bag frozen chopped spinach, thawed and squeezed dry

Preheat the oven to 350°F.

Season chicken with 1 teaspoon salt and ½ teaspoon black pepper, then dust with flour. In an ovenproof sauté pan, heat oil. Add chicken and sear each side for 3 to 4 minutes, until golden brown. Remove pan from heat.

In a small bowl, combine soup, mayonnaise, and lemon juice. Mix well.

Top each chicken breast with a mound of spinach and then nap each piece with the soup mixture. Bake uncovered for 45 to 50 minutes, until chicken is cooked through and sauce is bubbly and browned.

# MASHED CAULIFLOWER

*Serves 4 to 6*

1 head cauliflower, trimmed and cut into pieces

½ cup (1 stick) unsalted butter, plus more

2 teaspoons kosher salt

1 teaspoon coarse ground black pepper

⅓ cup grated Gruyère cheese,
plus additional for topping

In a large pot, steam cauliflower until fork tender. Drain and return to pot. Add ½ cup butter, salt, pepper, and cheese and mash with a potato masher until smooth. Transfer to an ovenproof serving dish and top with more cheese and dot with butter. Broil for 1 minute.

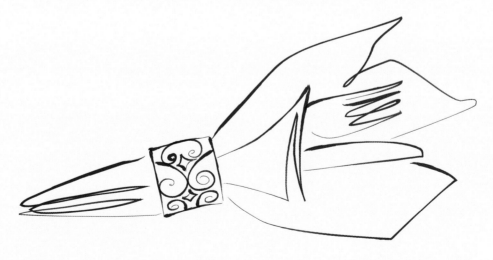

# Rib Roast Dinners

My parents were, and still are, what I call "cocktail intellectuals." They were active in business and in the community, and loved to entertain. They had a wide circle of friends and were never clique-ish. Guests came from a variety of sources: "the old gang"—the married children of my grandparents' contemporaries—people who grew up and raised their families in West Hartford, professional associates (my dad was a Harvard-trained periodontist; my mom a realtor) and an ever-changing array of eccentrics (read: kooks) that seemed to gravitate to our family. There were artists, musicians, politicos, and especially fellow sportsmen from my dad's uber-athletic world—sailors, tennis and squash players, and skiers.

The dinner was never lavish, but certainly considered and, above all, gracious. Drinks and hors d'oeuvre were served in the mahogany-paneled library that sported a crackling fireplace in winter. My parents drank first gin and then vodka Gibsons in short, cut crystal glasses that magnified the cocktail onions.

There was a riff on Caesar salad made in the Nutone blender. It was delicious but, in retrospect, quite common, featuring iceberg lettuce and cherry tomatoes. And it was even better the second day, all chilly and wilted and practically predigested.

The main course was always roast prime rib of beef, a dish my mom truly perfected. She would stud the beast with cloves of garlic and rub it with a paste of kosher salt, black pepper and paprika. Our family was in the supermarket business, so we had easy access to fine meats and, better yet, custom butchery. My mom would order the roast carefully trimmed, with the rib bones separated and reapplied with twine for easy carving. She knew her oven, rarely used a meat thermometer and truly had the dish down to a science. Accompanying it would be tragic (but still delicious) canned potatoes roasted with the meat, and green beans amandine. Dinner was followed by a frozen, molded chocolate mousse thing and coffee, followed by after-dinner drinks and cordials in the living room.

As children, we were always included at the table, unlike so many other families who either fed the kids first or sent out for pizza. We were even allowed to taste wine. My mom's name is Gloria, so my dad thought it cute that our house wine should be Chateau Gloria, a respected St. Julien.

It was delicious, and to this day I still love it. And being a part of, and *loving*, those very grown-up dinner parties probably set me on my course as a serial entertainer.

# IDIOT'S PRIME RIB

*Serves 6*

1 (5½- to 6-pound) standing rib roast (3 ribs)

½ cup coarse salt

½ cup black pepper

Béarnaise Sauce (page 72)

Heat oven to 500°F.

Place roast bone side down in a heavy roasting pan. In a small bowl, combine salt and pepper; mix well. Rub the entire roast with the salt and pepper mixture.

Bake the roast for 5 minutes per pound. Turn oven off and leave roast untouched for 1 hour. Do not open the oven door. Remove roast from oven and tent with aluminum foil. Allow to rest for 15 minutes. Slice and serve.

# BÉARNAISE SAUCE

¼ cup cider vinegar

¼ cup vermouth

1 shallot, minced

1 teaspoon dried tarragon

3 egg yolks

1 tablespoon water

½ cup (1 stick) unsalted butter

In a small saucepan, combine vinegar, vermouth, shallot, and tarragon. Bring to a boil and reduce until almost dry. Remove from heat and add egg yolks and water; whisk vigorously. Return pan to medium heat and continue whisking until eggs start to thicken. Add butter 1 tablespoon at a time and continue whisking. If sauce "breaks," or separates, add another yolk.

Keep warm in a double boiler. Serve with prime rib, steak, grilled salmon, or practically anything.

# COUNTRY CLUB CHOCOLATE CAKE

*Serves 8 to 10*

1 pound best-quality semi-sweet dark chocolate

1 cup (2 sticks) butter

8 eggs, room temperature

Whole strawberries, for garnish

2 cups sweetened whipped cream

Preheat the oven to 325°F. Grease a springform pan and reinforce outside with foil to ensure a tight seal.

Combine chocolate and butter in a glass bowl. Melt in microwave for 1 minute at a time until smooth. Stir after each minute.

Using an electric mixer, beat eggs in a large bowl for 5 minutes, or until doubled in volume. Stir one-third of the eggs into the chocolate to lighten it. Then add the chocolate mixture back to the remaining eggs and gently fold until well combined and the batter becomes chocolate colored.

Pour batter into the prepared springform pan. Create a bain marie (water bath) by setting the cake pan inside a large roasting pan.

*continued>*

Place both on the pulled-out middle oven rack. Pour boiling water into the roaster to come about halfway up the side of the springform pan. Bake at 325°F for 40 minutes. Cake should be firm to the touch without cracking.

Remove from oven and cool on a cooling rack, then refrigerate for at least 1 hour.

Remove the sides of the springform pan and place the cake on a cake platter. Decorate with whole strawberries. To serve, slice cake into wedges and place on individual dessert plates. Pass with a beautiful large bowl filled with whipped cream.

# SORTA STRAWBERRIES ROMANOFF

*Serves 4*

1 pint vanilla ice cream

1 pint fresh strawberries, hulled and quartered

1 cup sour cream

¼ cup brown sugar

½ teaspoon ground cinnamon

¼ cup orange liqueur
(e.g., Triple sec, Cointreau, Curaçao)

Fresh mint, for garnish

Divide ice cream among four goblets. Top with strawberries. Mix sour cream, brown sugar, and cinnamon together. Pour mixture over the strawberries, and splash each goblet with liqueur. Garnish with mint and serve immediately.

# Raising the Bar

I love a beautiful, well-stocked and inviting bar that's exposed and always at the ready. Not everyone likes this, especially families with young children or non-imbibers. But for our childless household, a prominent bar serves as a sort of welcome mat.

All of the units in our 1970s Palm Beach condo were equipped with wet bars near the entrance, and we use ours with gusto. It's a fun thing to decorate. Ours is behind louvered doors, so we can get away with a certain amount of shtick that doesn't have to be on view all of the time. I mean, carved coconut heads and framed cartoons and all of that kitschy shratt that one associates with good times.

There are limits, however. I don't want the interior of our bar to resemble an outpost of Spencer Gifts, that mall store full of junk that gave me the creeps just to walk by it, what with its Gay 90s "Bar's Open" lights and Lava Lamps and every possible kind of fiber optic thingy involving a beer can. A little humor is delightful, but there's a fine line leading into the territory of tasteless camp.

While I am not a big hard-liquor drinker, I do love the variety of bottles and shapes and colors that a bar involves. My advice is to always start with a nice big silver tray and build from there. A basic assortment consists of gin, rum, vodka, Scotch and bourbon. Add to that sweet and dry vermouth. If you want to go further, add Campari and perhaps a good tequila. For our Wisconsin bar, brandy and angostura bitters are essential for brandy old fashioneds, the local libation. Cranberry juice really needs to be refrigerated, so I bring it out in small quantities in a clear glass cruet. In a nearby cabinet, I keep club

soda, tonic and the inexpensive red and white French table wines that I like to serve for cocktails. If you are fond of cosmopolitans, you will need Rose's lime juice and Triple Sec or some other form of orange liqueur.

From the above assortment, you can create pretty much any drink, including nonalcoholic mocktails that are pretty without being potent.

For glasses, I prefer quantity over quality. While I love our heavy etched crystal double old fashioneds and delicate stemware, it's the dumb all-purpose bubble wine glasses that get used the most and seem to hold up the best. Splurge for several dozen and you will never worry about having enough for last-minute get-togethers.

Now, buy a good sturdy corkscrew, an attractive martini shaker, some kind of simple ice bucket, a metal scoop and, most importantly, a big metal wine chiller that can be filled with ice for larger crowds. I love my silver-plated one that looks like a party the minute I put it out.

One last thought: Don't be afraid to hire a bartender. For gatherings over twenty people, it allows you to be a gracious host and actually enjoy your own party rather than being a slave to it. In large cities, there are staffing services that feature unemployed actors and models that can truly charm your guests. They may not be the most efficient, but they sure are easy on the eyes and can help set the tone. If you belong to a club, ask the manager if any of the staff are allowed to moonlight. If there's a bar or restaurant you frequent, ask the bartender, as good bartenders always know others.

Frequent guests to our house know that even with a great bartender and other helpers, I still roam a cocktail party pouring wine or passing hors d'oeuvre. While I truly think it's a nice touch, the reality is that I just can't help myself.

# THE FAMILY WAY

Dining together as a family is a convention of life that is extremely important to the Stolmans. Early on, my parents insisted on everyone being together at the breakfast table before school. And, like any family with several kids, there was always an issue with who was brooding, who was fighting with whom and who was on what diet. But regardless of anyone's particular state of mind or appetite, breakfast was a command performance, complete with little footed cobalt-blue juice glasses and eggs served up on my mom's favorite Wedgewood breakfast set.

The same held true for dinner. We ate together as a family pretty much every night, and we ate what was put in front of us, from lamb chops to liver, without complaints. But on holidays, especially Jewish holidays, the food took on a special significance, as if partaking of the gefilte fish, matzo ball soup and potato kugel was keeping the faith alive.

To this day, I enjoy the rigors of a traditional Jewish holiday meal, albeit a lighter one with a few contemporary twists. I have done grand Rosh Hashanah dinners, lively Break Fasts and spirited Hanukkah feasts. But no dinner compares with a Passover Seder in significance or complexity. In our family, it's a heady mix of tradition and endurance, although gone are the days of the seemingly endless Hebrew-only Seders that I recall from my childhood. Back then, my grandmother would turn the great big dining table around so that it extended all the way into the living room to seat as many people as possible. To a child, it seemed as long as a bowling alley, as did the distance between the first blessing and the first course. My grandfather would always lead the service, as prescribed by the strict

Haggadah that was enigmatically published by the Maxwell House coffee company. The wine was very sweet, and even though we kids diluted ours with club soda to make it palatable, it made for a very drowsy headache.

Now that my parents live nearby in Florida, and we've all gotten a bit—*ahem*—older and smarter, our family Seders are far more contemporary. There's still my mother's perfect matzo ball soup and my grandfather's sterling silver Kiddush cup, but, thankfully, most of the service is recited in English. These days, even my dad, known for his intellectual intensity, manages to wrap it up in about a half hour. Now that's what I call progress!

# NANA'S MATZO BALLS

*Serves 6 to 8*

4 eggs

2 tablespoons vegetable oil or chicken fat

¼ cup seltzer

1 cup matzo meal

Kosher salt

Coarse ground black pepper

Water or chicken stock

Chicken soup, hot

Chopped dill, for garnish

In a medium bowl, whisk together the eggs, oil, and seltzer. Add the matzo meal and season with salt and pepper to taste. Stir well. Cover and refrigerate for several hours.

Bring a large pot of salted water or chicken stock to a boil. Wet hands and form mixture into golf ball–size matzo balls. Place matzo balls in the boiling liquid. Cover and reduce to a simmer. Cook for 30 minutes, or until soft and cooked through.

Remove with a slotted spoon and drain on a clean kitchen towel. Transfer to a pot of hot chicken soup and warm the matzo balls through. Serve one per person and garnish with chopped dill.

# CABBAGE STRUDEL

*Makes 4 strudels*

½ cup (1 stick) butter

1 head green cabbage, grated

½ cup brown sugar

2 teaspoons white wine vinegar

2 teaspoons salt

½ teaspoon pepper

½ cup breadcrumbs

1 (1-pound) box phyllo dough, thawed

1½ cups (3 sticks) butter, melted

Preheat the oven to 375°F.

In a large sauté pan, melt ½ cup butter over medium-high heat. Sauté cabbage until soft. Add brown sugar, vinegar, salt, and pepper. Continue cooking until most of the liquid is absorbed. Stir in breadcrumbs and cool.

Grease a sheet pan and set aside.

On a clean work surface, place a sheet of phyllo down. (Make sure to keep the other sheets covered with plastic wrap to prevent drying out.) Brush melted butter on the phyllo. Repeat with 4 more sheets, making a stack of buttered phyllo. Place a quarter of the filling along the long edge of the dough. Fold sides in and roll up. Place strudel on the sheet pan. Make 3 more strudels in the same manner, using all the phyllo and all the filling.

Bake for 25 to 30 minutes, until golden and flaky. Cut into 2-inch slices for a luncheon dish and smaller for hors d'oeuvre.

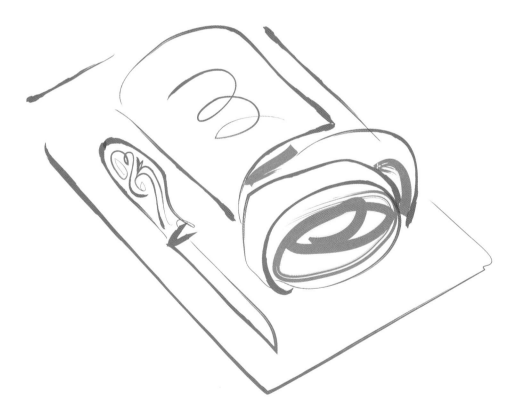

# COOKIE'S OVEN POTATO KUGEL

*Serves 8 to 10*

$^1/_2$ cup vegetable oil

6 large potatoes, peeled and cut into chunks

$1^1/_2$ large onions, quartered

5 eggs

$2^1/_4$ teaspoons salt

$^1/_2$ teaspoon white pepper

$^1/_2$ cup potato starch

Preheat the oven to 375°F.

Pour oil into a 9 x 13-inch glass casserole dish. Heat the dish in the oven until you are ready to pour the potato mixture into it.

Meanwhile, using a food processor with the grating disk, grate potatoes. Transfer to a colander and rinse under cold water until the water runs clear.

Switch to the steel "S" blade in the food processor. Process the onions for 6 to 8 seconds; add eggs, salt, and pepper and process for a few more seconds. Add the potatoes in batches and pulse until mixture is smooth but still quite thick. Pour the mixture into a large bowl and add the potato starch, folding it in to thoroughly combine.

Remove the baking dish from the oven and pour the mixture into it. Spoon the excess oil from the corners of the casserole dish onto top of the mixture. Bake uncovered for 1 hour, or until well browned and crispy.

Note: Do not freeze. It ruins the kugel.

# NANA'S SKILLET POTATO KUGEL

*Serves 6 to 8*

6 medium russet potatoes, peeled
and cut into large wedges

1 small yellow onion, peeled and cut into large pieces

2 eggs

$\frac{1}{2}$ cup matzo meal

2 teaspoons kosher salt

$\frac{1}{2}$ teaspoon cracked black pepper

Vegetable oil

In a food processor fitted with the shredding disk, shred the potatoes and onion. Remove the potato mixture to a bowl and replace the shredding disk with the "S" blade. In batches, pulse the mixture for 10 to 15 seconds. Place the potato mixture in a strainer over a bowl and squeeze out all the liquid. The potato starch will settle to the bottom of the bowl.

Place potato mixture in a bowl and fold in eggs, matzo meal, salt, pepper, and a few tablespoons of the reserved potato starch. Mix well.

Pour 1 inch of vegetable oil into a cast-iron or heavy skillet. Heat over high heat until oil bubbles around a small bit of potato mixture, then carefully add the mixture into the hot oil. Spread the mixture evenly in the skillet for a large pancake. Let cook for 8 to 10 minutes, until the sides and bottom are golden brown and crisp. Carefully flip the kugel and cook for 7 to 8 minutes, until golden brown. Remove and drain kugel on a paper towel. Cut into wedges and serve. (Don't let Uncle Billy near it or it won't have any crispy edges left.)

This dish can be made ahead of time and frozen. Reheat at 400°F for 10 to 12 minutes, until heated through. There is no need to defrost.

# AUNT MARILYN'S CARROT RING

*Serves 4 to 6*

1 cup margarine

1/2 cup firmly packed
brown sugar

1 egg

1 cup freshly grated carrots

1/2 cup water

1¼ cups sifted all-purpose flour

1/2 teaspoon baking soda

1/2 teaspoon cinnamon

1/2 teaspoon salt

1 (9-ounce) package frozen
peas and pearl onions, cooked
according to package directions

Preheat the oven to 350°F. Grease a medium ring mold with nonstick spray.

In a large bowl, cream margarine and brown sugar together. Add the egg and mix well. Stir in carrots and water.

In a small bowl, combine flour, baking soda, cinnamon, and salt. Add the flour mixture to the carrot mixture and mix until combined. Pour into the ring mold and bake for 50 minutes, or until a toothpick inserted in the middle comes out clean.

Invert carrot ring onto a serving platter and fill center with peas and pearl onions.

# NOODLE PUDDING

*Makes a 9 x 13-inch pan*

4 ounces whipped cream cheese

2 cups cottage cheese

1 pint sour cream, plus
more for topping

5 large eggs

½ cup plus 2 tablespoons
sugar, divided

1 cup (2 sticks) butter,
melted and divided

1 pound wide egg
noodles, cooked

2 cups corn flake crumbs

Sour cream

Preheat the oven to 350°F degrees. Grease a 9 x 13-inch glass baking dish and set aside.

Place the cream cheese, cottage cheese, sour cream, eggs, ½ cup sugar, and ½ cup butter in the bowl of a food processor fitted with the steel blade. Pulse the mixture until smooth. Transfer to a large bowl and add the noodles; toss well and transfer to the baking dish.

In a small bowl, combine corn flake crumbs, remaining 2 tablespoons butter and 2 tablespoons sugar. Mix until crumbs are well coated. Sprinkle the crumbs evenly over the noodles. Bake for 1 hour, or until golden brown and mixture begins to bubble.

Allow the pudding to rest before cutting into squares. Serve each square topped with a dollop of sour cream.

# SWEET-AND-SOUR SALMON EN GELÉE

*Serves 6*

6 (4-ounce) salmon fillets

3 medium yellow onions, sliced

3 cups water

2 teaspoons kosher salt

1/2 cup freshly squeezed
lemon juice

1/2 cup white vinegar

2 tablespoons sugar

1 teaspoon pickling spice

1/4 teaspoon peppercorns

1 bay leaf

1 package unflavored gelatin

2 whole lemons, thinly sliced

To a large straight-sided sauté pan, add the salmon, onions, water, salt, lemon juice, vinegar, sugar, pickling spice, peppercorns, and bay leaf. Bring to a boil and reduce to a simmer. Cook for 20 to 25 minutes, until salmon is light pink and cooked through. Remove salmon and transfer to a large baking dish.

Strain the liquid from the sauté pan into a saucepot, and then add the gelatin. Dissolve the gelatin by bringing the liquid to a boil for 2 minutes. Pour the liquid over the salmon and top with sliced lemons. Cool to room temperature, cover, and refrigerate overnight. Serve cold.

# KAREN'S SPECIAL BAKED SHRIMP AND FETA

*Serves 4 to 6*

3 tablespoons olive oil

2 large onions, diced

2 cloves garlic, minced

1 tablespoon chopped fresh dill

2 (28-ounce) cans chopped tomatoes

2 pounds raw shrimp, peeled and deveined

12 ounces crumbled feta cheese

½ cup chopped fresh parsley

Juice of 1 lemon

Preheat the oven to 450°F.

In a large straight-sided sauté pan, heat oil over medium-high heat. Add onion, garlic, and dill and cook until soft. Add tomatoes. Bring to a boil and reduce to a simmer. Continue cooking for 25 minutes, or until thickened. Stir in shrimp and cook for 5 minutes.

Spoon shrimp mixture into a 9 x 13-inch baking dish. Top with feta and bake for 10 to 15 minutes, until cheese is melted and bubbly. Sprinkle with parsley and lemon juice just before serving.

# AUNT TRINA'S CHICKEN

*Serves 6*

6 boneless, skinless chicken breasts

1 teaspoon salt

$1/2$ teaspoon coarse ground black pepper

$1/3$ cup all-purpose flour

3 eggs, beaten

$1/2$ cup vegetable oil

2 tablespoons olive oil

1 yellow onion, diced

3 cloves garlic, minced

8 ounces sliced Baby Bella mushrooms

$1/2$ cup dry white wine

$1/2$ cup chicken stock

1 (14-ounce) can quartered artichokes

$1/2$ cup chopped fresh parsley, for garnish

Preheat the oven to 350°F.

Season chicken with salt and pepper.

Place the flour in a medium bowl. In another medium bowl, beat the eggs. Dredge the chicken first in flour and shake off any excess, then dip the chicken in the egg.

Heat a large sauté pan with vegetable oil over medium-high heat. Place the chicken in the oil and cook for 3 to 4 minutes, until golden. Turn chicken over and cook for another 3 to 4 minutes. Transfer chicken to a sheet pan and bake in the oven until cooked through.

Meanwhile, in a large sauté pan, heat the olive oil. Add onion and cook for 3 to 4 minutes, until soft. Add garlic and mushrooms and cook for 4 to 5 minutes, until mushrooms are golden brown. Deglaze with the wine and stock. Stir in the artichokes and reduce sauce until it is slightly thickened.

Plate the chicken on a large platter; pour sauce over the chicken and sprinkle with parsley.

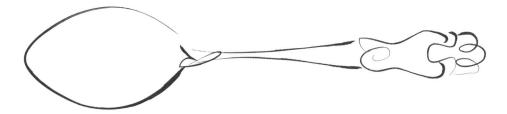

# DRUNKEN BRISKET

*Serves 10 to 12*

1 (4–4½-pound) brisket
(first cut preferred)

Kosher salt

Coarse ground black pepper

Canola oil

2 large yellow onions, sliced

2 large red onions, sliced

10 cloves garlic, sliced

1 package onion soup mix

1 bottle hearty red wine, such as
a Côtes du Rhône or Bordeaux

Preheat the oven to 350°F.

Season brisket with salt and pepper. In a large heavy-bottomed skillet with a scant bit of oil, sear brisket for 5 to 6 minutes on each side, until golden brown; remove the brisket and set aside.

Heat a few more tablespoons of oil in the same pan. Add onions and garlic. Cook over medium heat for 20 to 25 minutes, until golden and caramelized, then stir in the soup mix and wine. Stir well to gather the brown bits at the bottom of the pan.

Place half the onion mixture in a medium roasting pan, then top with brisket and remaining onions. Cover tightly with heavy-duty aluminum foil. Bake for 4 hours, or until fork tender.

Remove the meat from the oven and let rest, covered, for 10 minutes before slicing against the grain. Degrease the sauce by spooning out excess fat, then serve over the brisket.

# PUMPKIN CAKE

*Serves 8 to 10*

2 cups sifted all-purpose flour

2 teaspoons baking powder

1 teaspoon baking soda

$1/2$ teaspoon salt

$1^1/2$ teaspoon cinnamon

$1/2$ teaspoon cloves

$1/4$ teaspoon allspice

$1/4$ teaspoon ginger

4 eggs

2 cups sugar

1 (15-ounce) can pure pumpkin

1 cup vegetable oil

1 cup Kellogg's All-Bran cereal

1 (12-ounce) package semi-sweet chocolate chips

1 cup chopped walnuts

Powdered sugar, for garnish

Preheat the oven to 350°F. Grease a large Bundt pan and set aside.

In a large bowl, combine the flour, baking powder, baking soda, salt, cinnamon, cloves, allspice, and ginger.

In another large bowl, whisk the eggs until frothy. Add the sugar, pumpkin, oil, and cereal. Combine the pumpkin mixture with the flour mixture and stir until well blended. Stir in the chocolate chips and walnuts. Pour the batter into the prepared Bundt pan. Bake for 1 hour, or until a toothpick inserted in the middle comes out clean.

Dust with powdered sugar when cooled.

## Foraging in the Fridge, Freezer and Pantry

One of the greatest challenges for any home cook is to make a meal from whatever one has on hand. It's too tempting to plan a dinner, make a list and then go shopping for the necessary ingredients. And if you are like any typical New Yorker, your fridge contains little more than mustard, Worcestershire sauce and leftover Chinese food.

But in Palm Beach and Milwaukee, where we have real kitchens with real storage space, we actually go to the supermarket with the intent of outfitting our larder for more than one meal, and especially for last-minute unplanned guests. I think this is how most people who don't have small kitchens shop. For me, the basics of being prepared are to always have the following items on hand:

- Dijon mustard
- Cider Vinegar
- Extra virgin olive oil
- Shallots
- Mayonnaise
- Peeled, vacuum-packed hard-boiled eggs
- Shredded Swiss cheese
- Brown rice
- Low-sodium chicken stock
- Frozen chopped spinach
- Pasteurized egg substitute
- Penne or ziti pasta
- Grated Parmesan cheese
- Dried thyme, basil, oregano, rosemary
- Garlic powder, cayenne pepper, nutmeg, saffron
- A glamorous sea salt (I splurge on this)
- Coarse ground black pepper
- Hot pepper sauce
- Frozen boneless, skinless chicken thighs
- Frozen cooked shrimp
- Frozen whole wheat dinner rolls
- Butter (in freezer)
- Box of chopped tomatoes
- Good-quality ice cream

You will be totally amazed at what you can make from this with the addition of a head of lettuce and some milk if you can manage. From risotto to lush pasta dishes to egg soufflés to crispy roast chicken, you will never be caught off guard.

# THE BEST TABLE IN TOWN

◆◆◆

One day in the late '90s, when I had my resort wear shop on Worth Avenue in Palm Beach, a gorgeous antique Mercedes sports car pulled up in front of the store. It was navy blue with a red leather interior and, most unusually, had a white steering wheel. Equally stunning was the gal driving—a tall, sporty blonde in a white tennis dress with her sunglasses pushed up into her hair.

She introduced herself as "Pauline" and, in time, I learned that she grew up in a world of big houses all over the place, fully staffed. Yet, as I got to know her, I found her to be the most low-key and gentle of hostesses; maybe it was because she didn't have to impress anybody. Dinners at her house became something I looked forward to more than anything else, and that's where I learned the art of simplicity and an appreciation for good old home-style food, even on the most highbrow occasions.

Cocktail hours were kept short, a maximum of 45 minutes, and there was never an overabundance of hors d'oeuvre—maybe Lit'l Smokies with brown mustard or pieces of caramelized bacon passed on a silver platter. Dinner menus were uncluttered: things like macaroni and cheese, chicken hash, big platters of perfectly grilled lamb chops or chicken piccata with risotto and string beans. But, oh, that food! You have never tasted food as good or in such plentitude. And it was all beautifully served by a squadron of wonderful waiters, on large platters from which you would help yourself. I always loved how she would apologize to whomever was being served last for being seated in "starvation corner."

In tribute to Pauline's extraordinary hospitality, I've developed this repertoire. Now, all one needs to duplicate one of those sublime dinners is a menu culled from these recipes, a gorgeous, gracious house, fascinating dinner guests and a heart of gold.

# CARAMELIZED BACON

*Serves 8 to 10*

1 pound center-cut bacon

1½ cups firmly packed brown sugar

Coarse ground black pepper

Preheat the oven to 425°F.

Dry bacon well with a paper towel. Place sugar in a shallow dish. Coat the bacon with sugar on each side, making sure to press sugar onto the bacon. Sprinkle each side with black pepper.

Cover a sheet pan with parchment paper. Place the bacon on the sheet pan and bake for 10 minutes. Turn the bacon over and continue cooking for 8 to 10 minutes more, until bacon is shiny and golden. Be careful not to cook too long and burn the bacon.

Remove pan from oven and allow bacon to cool for 5 minutes. Transfer to a lightly greased sheet pan to further avoid sticking. Once bacon has hardened, break into pieces. Serve unadorned on your loveliest silver tray.

# PALM BEACH CHEESE PUFFS

### *Makes 6 dozen*

1 loaf Pepperidge Farm white sandwich bread

½ cup olive oil

¾ cup mayonnaise

¾ cup finely grated Parmesan cheese

1 tablespoon grated sweet onion

*350*

Preheat the oven to 375°F.

With a ½-inch round cookie cutter, cut rounds from slices of bread. Place bread rounds on a half sheet pan lined with parchment paper and brush with oil. Bake in the oven for 8 to 10 minutes, until golden. Transfer rounds to a cooling rack. *8 min*

Mix mayonnaise, cheese, and onion in a small bowl. Place cheese mixture in a pastry bag, or use a ziplock bag and snip the corner. Pipe onto each round. Bake at 375°F for 15 minutes, until golden and bubbly. *@ 7pm* *350*

Serve on a round glass dish or silver tray with a paper doily.

# CREAMED SPINACH

*Serves 4 to 6*

2 boxes frozen chopped spinach

¼ cup (½ stick) unsalted butter

2 shallots, minced

2 tablespoons flour

1 cup half & half

Pinch of sugar

Nutmeg

Salt and freshly ground black pepper

Thaw spinach and squeeze dry. There is no need to precook the spinach, as it cooks quickly in the following cream sauce.

Melt butter in a heavy-bottom saucepan over medium-high heat until the foaming subsides. Sauté shallots until soft. Add flour and continue cooking for 1 to 2 minutes. Slowly whisk in half & half. Continue cooking until mixture has thickened. Stir in spinach and add sugar. Season to taste with nutmeg and salt and pepper.

# Everybody Loves My Salad

I have friends who pride themselves on their carefully composed salads. They go to great lengths to impress with things like esoteric baby lettuces, artisanal arugulas and additions of horrifying items like watermelon, quinoa and various beets of the world. Ugh.

I come from a very different place. You must understand that I have never met a salad bar that I didn't like, and I truly believe that Green Goddess dressing is indeed god-like. So it is ironic that the salad that has become my go-to and hands-down crowd pleaser is incredibly simple and classic. It began with eating often at a wonderful French bistro in the unlikely location of Wauwatosa, Wisconsin. But there, at Le Reve on Harwood Avenue, I fell in love with their basic Demi Salad. It's just butter lettuce—but every leaf perfect and unblemished and bone dry—with the most amazing shallot vinaigrette. That's it. No croutons, no crumbles of blue cheese, no nothing. And it is absolutely delicious and addictive.

So this is the salad that I serve at almost every meal. I pride myself on making a proper, balanced vinaigrette, although I have a tendency to use too much. One day, perhaps with a bit more practice, I will learn some restraint and make my other half a happier camper. Meanwhile, the recipe follows, on the next page.

# BASIC FRENCH SALAD

*Serves 4 to 6*

2 heads butter lettuce, washed and dried

1 shallot, minced

1 tablespoon Dijon mustard

¼ cup cider vinegar

¾ cup olive oil

Salt and freshly ground black pepper

Remove lettuce leaves, then wash and dry them. Tear gently into bite-size pieces. Divide among individual salad plates. Set aside.

In a small glass jar with lid, combine the shallot, mustard, vinegar, olive oil, and salt and pepper to taste and screw lid on tightly. Shake until thoroughly mixed and emulsified.

Drizzle lightly over perfectly washed and dried leaves of lettuce. Toss gently and finish with a final bit of salt and pepper.

That's it. Truly.

# Gluten–Shmuten

When did everyone become so sensitive about gluten? Or peanuts? I mean, wasn't it just yesterday that we were shoving spoonfuls of peanut butter into our faces as a low-carb afternoon pick-me-up? Or starting every Chinese meal with cold sesame noodles, which is just another vehicle for consuming mass quantities of Skippy?

Bread and pasta have always been low on my list of desirables, from a weight-control point of view, but when did they suddenly become Enemy Number One?

And how do you explain San Francisco, which practically survives on spectacular sourdough bread? Or Italy, for that matter?

I believe that when one is preparing one's own food, it's fine to be as persnickety as one wishes. Every little allergy or sensitivity or dislike can be addressed privately and effectively. But when one is an invited guest and makes such a big deal about their food rules, I tend to believe that it's really one big smokescreen for a lack of sparkling wit. A little nibble won't hurt you, and it's easy to push food around until the plates are cleared. Children do it all the time. My wonderful grandfather found religion later in life and became kosher just as everyone else was discovering shrimp with lobster sauce. But he never complained and never explained. He simply brought along a cream cheese sandwich in his pocket.

# PENNE CARBONARA

*Serves 6*

1 pound dried penne pasta

½ pound bacon or
pancetta, diced

½ cup (1 stick) unsalted butter

2 cups half & half

2 egg yolks

1 cup grated Parmesan cheese

2 cups frozen peas

Salt and freshly ground
black pepper

Bring a large pot of salted water to a boil and cook the pasta until al dente. Drain the pasta, but do not rinse it.

In a large sauté pan, cook bacon or pancetta until crisp; remove from the pan and drain on paper toweling. Dispose of all grease and wipe the skillet dry. Melt butter and add half & half. Bring mixture to a rapid boil. Add pasta, reduce heat to low, and stir in the egg yolks. As the mixture begins to thicken, add the cheese, peas, and reserved bacon. Toss to combine, and season to taste with salt and pepper.

Serve immediately.

Variation: To make a cheesy casserole, transfer pasta mixture to a buttered casserole dish and top with more Parmesan cheese and dots of butter. Bake at 350°F for 20 minutes, or until the top is browned.

# CHICKEN MILANESE

*Serves 6*

6 boneless, skinless chicken breast halves

Kosher salt

Coarse ground black pepper

1/3 cup flour

1 1/2 cups seasoned breadcrumbs

1/4 cup grated Parmesan cheese

2 large eggs, beaten

Canola oil

Chopped parsley, for garnish

Lemon slices, for garnish

On a clean work surface, pound chicken to 1/2 inch thick. Season each side with salt and pepper.

Place flour in a shallow dish. Combine breadcrumbs and Parmesan and place in another shallow dish. Place beaten eggs in a bowl. Dredge chicken in flour and shake off the excess, dip into the eggs, and then dredge with breadcrumbs.

Heat 1/2 inch of oil in a large sauté pan over medium-high heat. Add chicken and cook for 4 to 6 minutes on each side. Make sure chicken is browned and cooked through.

Transfer to a platter and garnish with chopped parsley and lemon slices. Serve chicken with Saffron Orzo with Peas (page 114).

# SAFFRON ORZO WITH PEAS

*Serves 6 to 8*

4 cups low-sodium chicken broth

2 quarts water

Salt

1 teaspoon saffron threads

1 (16-ounce) box orzo pasta

1 tablespoon extra virgin olive oil

4 cups (16 ounces) frozen peas

1 cup grated Parmesan cheese

Coarse salt

Coarse ground black pepper

Pinch of nutmeg

Heat chicken broth, 2 quarts salted water, and saffron threads to boiling in a large pot. Add orzo and cook until al dente—just tender with a bit of a bite. Drain and return to pot.

Add olive oil and peas, and cover to allow peas to warm up. Just before serving, add Parmesan cheese and a dash of salt, pepper, and nutmeg.

Serve immediately.

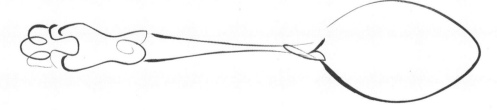

# I Hate Hostess Gifts

Okay, this one is going to make enemies, as I have many wonderful friends who own delicious little shops or Websites that sell the nicest things.

But there is nothing more depressing to me than having to deal with a hostess gift. It's gotten so competitive, what with fancy scented candles, kooky coasters and cutesy books that are now practically the price of admission to a good party. I mean, what happened to the bottle of wine and a nice thank-you note?

There was a time in Palm Beach when the hostess gift de rigueur among a certain set was this charming little carriage clock from Tiffany & Co. It cost something like $500. Isn't that just the stupidest thing you've ever heard of? At that price, I want to just stay home.

My biggest pet peeve is the guest who arrives with a big bunch of fresh flowers and expects you to drop everything and arrange them. I have been on panel discussions with other entertaining experts and just can't get off this topic. Don't you wish there could be some kind of chute by the front door to throw these floral tributes down immediately? Just seeing the guest's expression would be the best hostess gift in the world.

Lest you think I'm just an awful curmudgeon, the one thing I do find so appreciated is the post-party gesture. It could be a little bunch of flowers, a handwritten note or, honestly, a heartfelt email. It's the guests who take the time to express their thanks for all the hard work that goes along with entertaining who definitely get invited back. It amazes me how few seem to understand this tiny little thing.

# ONE BOWL GINGERBREAD CAKE

*Makes 1 Bundt cake*

4 eggs

1 cup firmly packed light brown sugar

$^2/_3$ cup molasses

1 cup vegetable oil

2$^1/_2$ cups all-purpose flour

1 tablespoon baking powder

$^1/_2$ teaspoon salt

$^1/_4$ teaspoon baking soda

2 teaspoons ground ginger

$^1/_2$ teaspoon cinnamon

$^1/_4$ teaspoon nutmeg

$^1/_4$ teaspoon allspice

Powdered sugar, for garnish

Applesauce, for serving

Whipped cream, for serving

Preheat the oven to 350°F. Grease a 10-cup Bundt pan and set aside.

In a large bowl, beat eggs lightly with a whisk, then whisk in brown sugar, molasses, and oil. Add flour, baking powder, salt, baking soda, ginger, cinnamon, nutmeg, and allspice and mix to combine. Do not overmix or the gingerbread will be tough. Pour into the prepared pan and bake for 30 to 40 minutes, until an inserted toothpick comes out clean. Let cake cool for 10 minutes, then invert onto a cooling rack.

Dust with powdered sugar before serving. Serve with applesauce and whipped cream on the side.

# WINTER DINNERS

◆◆◆

Winters growing up in New England were rather nasty. Don't get me wrong: there was a certain charm to blankets of newly fallen snow, along with that eerie quiet that would invariably follow a big blizzard. And then there were the vicious ice storms that would glaze every tree limb in shimmering splendor but would also send them crashing to the ground from the added weight, taking down power lines, of course. During those gray and white days and long, dark nights, we'd make a big fire in the library and wait for the electricity, and more importantly the TV, to come back on. Food certainly helped to while away the hours.

I actually love big, hearty winter dinners. It's ironic that I would end up spending so much time in Palm Beach, where stews and casseroles make about as much sense as fur coats. But now that I have a home in Wisconsin, I've had to revisit my repertoire of rib-sticker dishes. I must say, it's a treat to once again build roaring fires and put out things like meatloaf and chicken potpie and have people actually like it. After all, the last thing on anyone's mind in mid-winter Milwaukee is how one is going to look in a bathing suit the following day.

# BROCCOLI PURÉE

*Serves 4 to 6*

6 cups broccoli florets

½ cup (1 stick) unsalted butter

Pinch of sugar

Nutmeg

Salt

Freshly ground black pepper

In a large pot, steam the broccoli until tender; drain. Transfer to a food processor fitted with a steel blade. Add the butter and pulse until smooth. Add sugar and season to taste with nutmeg, salt, and pepper.

Note: This is the perfect accompaniment to any simple meat, chicken, or fish entrée.

# TOMATO PUDDING

*Serves 6*

³/₄ cup (1¹/₂ sticks) unsalted butter, divided (1 stick
for melting and ¹/₂ stick for dotting top of pudding)

1 (26-ounce) carton Pomì chopped tomatoes

1 tablespoon dried thyme

Salt and freshly ground black pepper

6 slices whole wheat bread

Grated Parmesan cheese

Preheat the oven to 375°F. Butter a 10-inch round casserole dish and set aside.

Melt ¹/₂ cup of butter in a small saucepan. Add the tomatoes and thyme, and season to taste with salt and pepper.

Tear the bread into medium-size chunks and place in a large bowl. Add tomato mixture and toss to coat. Pour pudding into the casserole dish. Sprinkle the top with cheese and dot with remaining ¹/₄ cup butter. Bake for 30 minutes, or until beautifully puffed and browned.

Note: For whatever reason, this dish holds heat like a nuclear reactor. Use caution when serving.

# CHICKEN POTPIE WITH AN HERBED BISCUIT CRUST

*Serves 8*

2 pounds boneless, skinless chicken breasts

2 cups chicken broth

1 cup dry vermouth

1/2 cup (1 stick) unsalted butter

4 leeks, cleaned and julienned

1/2 cup all-purpose flour

1 pint half & half

Salt and freshly ground black pepper

2 cups baking mix, such as Bisquick

1 cup milk

2 eggs

1 tablespoon dried thyme

Preheat the oven to 400°F. Grease a large baking dish and set aside.

In a large sauté pan, poach chicken in broth and vermouth by bringing liquid to a boil, adding chicken, and reducing heat to a simmer. When chicken is cooked through, after about 20 minutes, remove from the poaching liquid and reserve the liquid. Let the chicken cool, then shred it into bite-size pieces.

Melt the butter in a sauté pan over medium-high heat and cook leeks until golden. Sprinkle leeks with flour and cook for 3 to 4 minutes while stirring continuously. Add reserved poaching liquid and half & half. Whisk until mixture is thickened and free of lumps.

Season mixture with salt and pepper to taste. Fold in chicken.
Combine well and pour into the baking dish.

In a large bowl, combine the baking mix, milk, eggs, and thyme.
Cover chicken mixture with dough and bake for 30 minutes, or until
golden brown.

# HURRY-UP COQ AU VIN

*Serves 6 to 8*

8 boneless, skinless chicken thighs

¼ cup all-purpose flour

1 teaspoon kosher salt

½ teaspoon coarse ground black pepper

Canola oil

8 ounces slab bacon, diced

8 ounces baby carrots

3 cloves garlic, minced

8 ounces frozen pearl onions, thawed

1 quart whole white mushrooms, brushed clean

1 tablespoon tomato paste

2 cups dry red wine

2 bay leaves

1 teaspoon dried thyme

A slurry of 1 tablespoon cornstarch
mixed with a little water

½ cup chopped parsley, for garnish

Place chicken in a large bowl. In a separate bowl, combine flour, salt, and pepper; mix well. Pour the flour mixture over the chicken and coat well.

In a large Dutch oven, heat approximately a 1/8-inch depth of oil over medium-high heat. In batches, brown the chicken on both sides and transfer to a plate. Add the bacon and cook until crispy, then remove and reserve.

Preheat the oven to 350°F.

To the same Dutch oven, add the carrots, garlic, onions, and mushrooms. Cook for 3 to 4 minutes, until all ingredients take on some color and brown lightly. Stir in the tomato paste and deglaze with the red wine, scraping any brown bits from the bottom of the pan. Add the reserved chicken and bacon to the pot along with bay leaves and thyme. Bring to a simmer, cover, and bake for 45 minutes to 1 hour, until chicken is tender.

Remove from oven and return to stove on medium-high heat. Add slurry to slightly thicken sauce. Garnish with chopped parsley before serving.

# KINDA CASSOULET

*Serves 6 to 8*

1 pound boneless, skinless chicken thighs

¹/₄ cup all-purpose flour

1 teaspoon salt, plus additional for seasoning

¹/₂ teaspoon coarse ground black pepper,
plus additional for seasoning

¹/₂ cup light olive oil plus 1 tablespoon, divided

1 pound turkey kielbasa

1 medium onion, chopped

3 cloves garlic, chopped

1 cup chicken stock

¹/₄ cup plus 2 tablespoons dry vermouth, divided

1 (14-ounce) can cannellini beans, drained and rinsed

1 cup whole wheat breadcrumbs

¹/₄ cup chopped parsley

Preheat oven to 350°F.

Pat chicken thighs dry.

In a small bowl, combine flour with 1 teaspoon salt and ½ teaspoon pepper. Season chicken thighs with salt and pepper, then dust with flour mixture and shake off excess.

In a large ovenproof sauté pan, heat 2 tablespoons light olive oil over medium-high heat and brown the chicken on both sides for 4 to 5 minutes per side. Remove the chicken from the pan and reserve. Add the turkey sausage and brown on both sides; remove sausage from the pan and reserve.

Pour 1 tablespoon of light olive oil into the same pan; add onion and cook over medium-high heat for 3 to 5 minutes, until golden. Add garlic and continue cooking for 1 minute. Deglaze the pan with chicken stock and ¼ cup vermouth. Add the chicken and sausage back into the pan. Stir in the beans and nestle the meat within the beans.

In a medium bowl, mix the breadcrumbs, ¼ cup olive oil, and parsley, and season with salt and pepper to taste. Place mixture on top of the beans and meat and drizzle with remaining 1 tablespoon light oil and 2 tablespoons vermouth.

Place the pan in the oven and bake for 45 minutes, or until cassoulet is bubbly and breadcrumbs are golden brown.

# ROAST CHICKEN PROVENÇAL

*Serves 6 to 8*

8 bone-in, skin-on chicken thighs

2 teaspoons kosher salt

1 teaspoon coarse ground black pepper

3/4 cup flour

3–4 tablespoons light olive oil

2 tablespoons herbs de Provence

1 lemon, quartered

10 cloves garlic, unpeeled

10 small shallots, peeled

1/3 cup dry vermouth

Thyme sprigs

Preheat oven to 375°F.

On a clean work surface, season the chicken with salt and pepper. Place the flour in a shallow dish and lightly dredge the chicken.

Place the chicken in a large roasting pan and season with herbs de Provence. Add lemon, garlic, shallots, and vermouth. Bake for 50 to 60 minutes, until chicken is very crispy and cooked through. Halfway through the cooking time, baste the chicken with the pan liquid.

Transfer to a large platter and garnish with full sprigs of thyme.

# COUNTRY CAPTAIN
# PORK CHOPS

*Serves 6 to 8*

2 cups all-purpose flour

1 teaspoon salt

1 teaspoon coarse
ground black pepper

8 (¹/₂-inch-thick)
boneless pork chops

¹/₃ cup canola oil

1 large onion, chopped

1 red bell pepper, chopped

1 green bell pepper, chopped

3 tablespoons curry powder

1 cup dry vermouth

2 cups Pomì chopped tomatoes

1 cup dried currants

1 cup slivered almonds

1 large bay leaf

Coconut rice (recipe follows)

Combine flour, salt, and pepper in a shallow bowl. Dredge chops in the flour and shake off the excess. Heat oil in a Dutch oven over medium-high heat, and brown both sides of the chops in batches. Remove chops from the pan and reserve.

Add onion and peppers to the Dutch oven and sauté over medium-high heat until soft. Add curry powder and cook until toasted, about 2 minutes. The fragrance will intensify.

Add the vermouth and deglaze the pan, scraping off any bits stuck to the bottom. Add the tomatoes and tuck chops into simmering liquid. Add currants, almonds, and bay leaf. Taste and correct seasonings as desired. Cover and simmer for 1 hour, or until chops are tender.

Serve over Coconut Rice.

## COCONUT RICE

1 can unsweetened coconut milk

1 can water (measure in the empty coconut milk can)

1 large pinch coarse salt

1 can brown rice (measure in empty coconut milk can

Pinch of red pepper flakes

Combine the coconut milk, water, and salt and bring to a boil. Add the rice and cover. Lower the heat and simmer until all liquid is evaporated and tiny holes appear. Uncover, sprinkle with pepper flakes, and fluff.

# TURKEY MEATLOAF

*Serves 4 to 6*

2 tablespoons vegetable oil

1 medium onion, diced

1/2 cup chopped celery

4 slices multigrain bread, torn into small pieces

1 cup milk, divided

2 eggs

2 tablespoons Worcestershire sauce

1 1/2 pounds ground turkey

1 teaspoon salt

1 teaspoon thyme

1/2 teaspoon coarse ground black pepper

1/2 pound sliced turkey bacon

Piquant Tomato Sauce (recipe on page 137)

Preheat oven to 350°F.

In a large sauté pan, heat the oil over medium-high heat. Sauté the onion and celery until soft and golden brown; set aside.

*continued>*

In a large bowl, soak bread in ½ cup milk. Whisk in eggs and Worcestershire sauce. Add sautéed vegetables, ground turkey, salt, thyme, and pepper. Mix until well combined.

In a large, lightly greased baking dish or roasting pan, form mixture into a loaf. Crisscross bacon slices and over the entire loaf. Pour Piquant Tomato Sauce over all. Cover with foil and bake for 1 hour. Remove foil and continue baking for 15 to 20 minutes, until the bacon is crispy and a meat thermometer inserted into the center of the loaf reads 165°F. Let rest for 10 minutes before slicing.

# PIQUANT TOMATO SAUCE

*Makes 1 1/2 cups*

2 tablespoons olive oil

1 medium onion, chopped

2 cloves garlic, chopped

2 tablespoons tomato paste

1 (26-ounce) carton Pomì chopped tomatoes

2 tablespoons cider vinegar

1 tablespoon chili powder

Pinch of sugar

Salt and freshly ground black pepper

In a medium saucepan, heat the oil over medium-high heat. Sauté the onion and garlic until soft and translucent. Stir in the tomato paste and cook for 1 minute. Add tomatoes, vinegar, chili powder, and sugar. Bring to a boil, and then reduce to a simmer. Continue cooking until sauce is thickened. Season to taste with salt and pepper.

# What to wear to a small dinner party

Ever since *Downton Abbey* hit America's shores, dressing for dinner has taken on a totally new meaning.

This isn't to say that people are running out and purchasing dressing gowns and piling on strands of jet beads and throwing marcasite combs in their hair, but there does seem to be a renewed interest in not only looking good at table, but also being rather engaging—even witty. I am all for this, considering the frightening commonality of an entire family seated at a dinner table, each one's eyes fixed on his or her own particular devices. Is there anything sadder?

While one should always attempt to dress attractively, dressing comfortably is equally important. A shirt with a tight collar or a sweater that itches certainly won't make you the most delightful dinner companion. Shoes that pinch or pants that restrict circulation—anything that incites an "ouch"—should be avoided. How can one be charming when one is in pain?

News anchors have always known the real secret: look great from the waist up; dress comfy below the desk. The same goes for dinner parties. And now, with comfy cozy things like velvet smoking slippers and trousers with stretch and jewelry that looks dramatic without weighing a ton, it's very easy to look dazzling without a lot of effort or money.

The thing is to simply *try*. Just as you want the plates set before you to be filled with something delicious, serve up your own kind of goodness with a pleasing appearance and some good conversation.

# NANCY DEVITA'S FISH STEW

*Serves 4*

1 pound boneless, skinless haddock or cod fillets

1½ cups water

1 teaspoon dill seed

1 can Campbell's Tomato Bisque

⅓ cup chopped parsley, divided

1 cup sour cream, divided

In a large straight-sided skillet, simmer the fish in water and dill seed until cooked through, about 10 minutes. Remove fish from the pan using a slotted spatula and allow to cool; the fish will naturally break up into smaller pieces.

To the fish stock, add the bisque, half of the parsley, and ½ cup sour cream. Mix well to dissolve. Add fish pieces along with half of the remaining parsley. Serve each bowl with a dollop of the remaining sour cream and an additional sprinkle of parsley.

# ALFRESCO

From late spring to early fall, we ate in the glassed-in porch overlooking a beautiful brick patio; we sat at a wrought-iron-and-glass dining set inherited from my Aunt Mildred's very grand house on Long Island. There was a trickling stone fountain—a little boy holding an urn—set among rhododendron and towering pines and the ever-present Charmglow gas grill. Here, dinner was my dad's domain, with a variety of grilled items that ran the gamut from suburban London broil to swordfish steaks brushed with anchovy paste.

# THE RUSTY PELICAN'S CASTAWAY SALAD

*Serves 4 to 6*

6 cups chopped romaine lettuce

2 hard-boiled eggs, chopped

1 pound baby shrimp, chilled

1 medium red onion, chopped

½ cup mayonnaise

2 tablespoons Dijon mustard

1 tablespoon honey

Salt and freshly ground black pepper

Place the lettuce in a large salad bowl. Add the eggs, shrimp, and onion.

In a medium bowl, whisk together mayonnaise, mustard, and honey.

At the table, add salad dressing with aplomb, poured from on high, and toss. Season to taste with salt and pepper and serve with chilled salad forks—essential!

# CHILLED ZUCCHINI SOUP

*Serves 6 to 8*

1 tablespoon olive oil

1 yellow onion, diced

2 pounds fresh zucchini, diced

1 tablespoon curry powder

4 cups low-sodium chicken broth

Salt and coarse ground black pepper

2% plain Greek yogurt, for garnish

In a large sauté pan, heat the oil over medium-high heat; add the onions and cook for 2 to 3 minutes, until soft and translucent. Add the zucchini and continue cooking until soft. Stir in the curry powder and cook for an additional 1 to 2 minutes.

Transfer the mixture to a food processor fitted with a steel blade and pulse the mixture until smooth. Add chicken stock as needed to thin the mixture to a bisque consistency. Season with salt and pepper to taste. Place in a covered container and cool for at least 2 hours or overnight in the refrigerator.

Serve with a dollop of Greek yogurt.

# STOVETOP POACHED SALMON

### *Serves 6 to 8*

½ cup sliced celery

½ cup diced shallots

½ lemon, sliced

2 cups dry white wine

4 cups water

2 teaspoons kosher salt

2 pounds skinless salmon fillets, cut into 6 pieces

Sour Cream Dill Sauce (recipe follows)

Sliced peeled cucumbers, for serving

In a straight-sided sauté pan or shallow pot, combine celery, shallots, lemon, wine, water, and salt. Bring to a boil and reduce to a simmer. Add salmon to poaching liquid. Cover and cook until salmon is cooked through and opaque.

Remove salmon with a slotted spatula and transfer to a serving platter. Refrigerate at least several hours, preferably overnight.

Serve with a dollop of Sour Cream Dill Sauce.

This is especially nice served with chilled, peeled, and sliced cucumbers, dressed with a little cider vinegar, sugar, and chopped dill.

## SOUR CREAM DILL SAUCE

1 cup sour cream

1 cup mayonnaise

1 tablespoon anchovy paste

2 tablespoons chopped dill

¼ cup Dijon mustard

Combine ingredients and mix well. Chill before serving.

# MY BOUILLABAISSE

*Serves 6 to 8*

Olive oil

1 large yellow onion, diced

1 teaspoon dried orange peel

Pinch of saffron

1 teaspoon dried thyme

$1/2$ cup dry vermouth

1 (8-ounce) bottle clam juice

1 (26-ounce) box Pomì chopped tomatoes

2 cloves garlic, mashed

1 pound cod fillets

1 pound red snapper fillets

Salt

Freshly ground black pepper

Red pepper flakes

1 bay leaf

2 dozen littleneck clams

2 dozen large shrimp, peeled and deveined, tails on

1 pound calamari, rings and tentacles

1 pound sea scallops

1 (4-ounce) jar roasted red peppers, drained

1 cup mayonnaise

6–8 generous slices French bread, toasted

4 cups shredded Gruyère cheese

Chopped parsley, for garnish

In a large Dutch oven, heat oil at $1/8$-inch depth over medium-high heat and sauté the onion until translucent. Add the orange peel, saffron, thyme, vermouth, clam juice, tomatoes, and garlic. Add cod

*continued>*

and red snapper, salt, pepper, red pepper flakes, and bay leaf. Simmer until the fish dissolves and thickens the soup.

Add the clams and cover tightly. As soon as clams open and moments before serving, add the shrimp, calamari, and scallops and cook until just opaque.

In a food processor fitted with a steel blade, pulse process red peppers and mayonnaise to make a rouille. It should be a smooth, coral-colored puree. Reserve.

Place a slice of toasted French bread in the bottom of each individual bowl. Add a dollop of the rouille and a large handful of shredded cheese. Ladle the soup over the bread and garnish with chopped parsley.

# SCALLOPED SCALLOPS

*Serves 6 to 8*

2 pounds bay scallops,
rinsed and patted dry

¹/₂ cup plus 2 tablespoons butter

¹/₂ cup diced onion

¹/₂ cup diced celery

1¹/₂ cups crushed Ritz crackers

¹/₄ cup vermouth

¹/₂ cup chopped
parsley, for garnish

Lemon wedges, for garnish

Preheat the oven to 450°F.

In a medium ovenproof baking dish that has been lightly greased, layer the scallops.

In a large sauté pan, melt ¹/₂ cup butter over medium-high heat. Add the onion and celery and cook until softened. Stir in the crackers and mix well.

Top the scallops with the cracker crumbs. Dot with remaining 2 tablespoons butter and splash with vermouth. Bake for 12 to 15 minutes, until scallops are cooked through and the topping is golden brown. Turn oven off and allow to sit for 5 to 8 minutes before serving.

Garnish with chopped parsley and lemon wedges.

# SIMPLE PAELLA

*Serves 6 to 8*

5 cups chicken stock

1 large pinch saffron threads

2 tablespoons vegetable oil

1 pound boneless, skinless chicken thighs

1 pound hot Italian turkey sausage

1 medium onion, diced

3 cloves garlic, minced

2 cups brown rice

1/2 cup white wine

1 dozen littleneck clams

1/2 pound calamari rings and tentacles

1/2 pound scallops

1/2 pound large shrimp, peeled and deveined

1 cup frozen green peas

1/4 cup diced red bell pepper

1/4 cup chopped parsley

In a medium pot, combine chicken stock and saffron. Bring to a boil, then remove from heat and allow to steep for 10 minutes.

In a large straight-sided sauté pan or paella pan, heat the oil over medium-high heat. Add the chicken thighs and brown on both sides. Remove and set aside. Add the sausage and sear on all sides. Remove and set aside. Add the onion and sauté for 2 to 3 minutes, until golden; add the garlic and continue cooking for 1 minute. Add the rice and stir to coat well. Deglaze the pan with white wine, scraping up the bits of brown stuck to the pan.

To the pan, add 4 cups of saffron-infused stock and return the chicken and sausage to the pan. Stir well and bring to a boil, then cover and allow to simmer for 25 to 30 minutes, or until rice is tender.

Remove cover and add clams. Cover and cook for 5 to 6 minutes, until shells begin to open. Add calamari, scallops, shrimp, peas, and diced pepper. Cook for an additional 6 to 8 minutes, until the seafood is cooked through. Sprinkle with parsley just before serving.

# GRILLED SWORDFISH MERRICK

*Serves 6*

6 medium swordfish steaks
(approximately 2¹/₂ pounds total)

¹/₂ cup (1 stick) butter

1 cup honey

1 cup soy sauce

1 tablespoon chopped garlic

1 tablespoon coarse ground black pepper

Lemon wedges

Trim swordfish steaks of all skin and fat, and place steaks in a 9 x 13-inch baking dish for marinating. In a medium saucepan over medium-high heat, melt the butter. Add the honey, soy sauce, garlic, and pepper; stir to combine. The warmth of the butter will thin out the honey. Pour over steaks and marinate in the refrigerator for at least 30 minutes. The butter will congeal. This is normal.

Preheat the grill to high heat and lightly oil the grates. Grill steaks (or, if a grill is not available, broil them in your oven) for 8 to 10 minutes on each side, until golden and cooked through. Serve with lemon wedges.

# Helping Out

Do you offer to help the host in the kitchen or not?

All of my kitchens, with the exception of the one in Milwaukee, are little more than aircraft galleys. And while I still manage to put out grand dinners for six or cocktails for a crowd from these small spaces, it does take a certain amount of choreography to accomplish these feats of culinary prowess. Basically, I cook and serve and my other half, Rich, clears and cleans. That way, one of us is always at the table keeping the dinner party going. And while I have a tendency to bounce up and down a lot, I try to at least remain visible. I have vivid memories of Friday-night dinners at my grandparents' house, where my nana's seat would remain unoccupied, as she, for whatever reason, could not tear herself away from the stove.

I prefer that guests remain guests and not try to help out. We end up bumping into each other, things get broken and, frankly, a lot of the hocus pocus that goes on in my kitchen is for my eyes only. No one needs to know about that extra fillip of butter that I might add to a sauce to make it yummy or the last-minute cornstarch save that I sometimes need to enact on a soup that's too thin. Julia Child said it best: "Remember, you are alone in the kitchen and nobody can see you." I fully intend to keep it that way.

# BREAKFAST

◆◆◆

We are "breakfast out" kind of people. Like my parents, Rich and I love nothing more than two seats at the counter of a good old greasy spoon. There is something about the aroma of coffee and bacon combined with the clatter of china and flatware. It also motivates us to hit the gym first, which is ironic since I was one of those kids that thought of gym as something to get *out* of rather than get *in* to. I must have forged my mother's signature a million times on a variety of excuses that ran the gamut from mononucleosis to a plantar wart that lasted two years.

But when we have weekend guests or are feeling domestic, especially in our suburban Milwaukee home, which has a proper kitchen, I have a small repertoire of breakfast dishes that seem to make people happy. Besides, there is no more gracious way to say good-bye to houseguests than to give them a sturdy breakfast before they get on the road.

# AUNT FLO'S PRALINE RING

*Makes 1 Bundt cake*

$\frac{1}{2}$ cup currants

$\frac{1}{4}$ cup dark rum

$\frac{1}{2}$ cup (1 stick) butter

$\frac{1}{2}$ cup chopped pecans, divided

$\frac{3}{4}$ cup firmly packed brown sugar

1 tablespoon water

2 (8-ounce) cans refrigerated crescent dinner rolls

Preheat the oven to 350°F.

Combine currants and rum in a small glass bowl and microwave for 3 minutes. Remove bowl from microwave and allow to sit so the currants can plump a bit.

Melt butter in a small saucepan. With a pastry brush, coat a 12-cup Bundt pan with melted butter. Sprinkle $\frac{1}{2}$ cup pecans and half of the currant mixture on the bottom; set pan aside.

To the remaining melted butter, add remaining $\frac{1}{2}$ cup pecans, brown sugar, and water. Bring to a boil, reduce to a simmer, and cook for 1 to 2 minutes, stirring occasionally.

Remove dough from cans and cut each roll into 8 slices, using the pre-scored marks as a guide. Place 8 slices cut side down in the Bundt pan, top with half the brown sugar mixture and the remaining half of the currant mixture. Place remaining dough slices on top, and spoon the remaining sugar mixture over the slices.

Bake for 30 to 35 minutes, until golden brown. Remove from the oven and let cool for 2 to 3 minutes. Invert onto a serving platter.

# CHRISTMAS MORNING MATZO BREI

*Serves 2 to 4*

4 boards of matzo

4 eggs

Peanut oil

Kosher salt

Run the matzo under hot water until dampened. Break into 1-inch pieces. In a large bowl, beat the eggs, then add the matzo and stir to coat well.

Pour $1/8$ inch of peanut oil into a large skillet and heat over medium-high until a bit of matzo sizzles; then add the matzo mixture. Fry the matzo while stirring constantly, until it is golden brown and the eggs are cooked through. Serve with a sprinkle of salt.

# TOAD IN THE HOLE

*Serves 2*

2 slices fresh challah or hearty multigrain bread

Butter, softened

2 large eggs

Kosher salt

Coarse ground black pepper

Grated Parmesan cheese

Ketchup

Place bread on a clean work surface. Lightly butter the bread on both sides. Cut out the center of each bread slice with a 2- to 2½-inch round cutter.

Heat a nonstick sauté pan over medium-high heat. Place bread in the pan. Crack an egg into the center of each bread slice. Cook the egg and bread for 2 to 3 minutes on one side. Carefully flip the egg and bread, and cook the other side until bread is golden brown and the egg has reached desired doneness. Season to taste with salt and pepper.

Serve with a sprinkling of Parmesan Cheese and a squiggle of ketchup.

# EGGS AU REVOIR

*Serves 4*

| | |
|---|---|
| 8 eggs | Freshly ground black pepper |
| 2 tablespoons butter | 4 slices buttered multigrain toast, for serving |
| 2 cups grated Parmesan cheese | |

Break eggs into a big bowl and whisk lightly until the yolks are broken and blended with the whites. Add a scant tablespoon of water. Do not add any salt, as it will toughen the eggs.

Heat a large nonstick skillet over medium-high heat. Add butter and melt until the foaming subsides. Add the eggs and begin stirring with a wooden spoon. Move skillet on and off the heat as necessary, being very careful not to overcook the eggs. At this point, you want the eggs to be significantly underdone.

When the eggs are halfway done, add the cheese and continue to stir. Take the skillet off the heat and use the residual heat of the pan to finish cooking the eggs and melting the cheese. Aim for a curdled hollandaise consistency. Add a great deal of pepper and transfer into 4 bowls.

Serve with rectangles of buttered multigrain toast for optimum dipping.

Do not garnish. Do not serve with bacon or sausage or—heaven forbid—fruit. The joy of this dish is its comforting simplicity.

# FOOLPROOF BREAKFAST CASSEROLE

### *Serves 8 to 10*

2 tablespoons vegetable oil

1 pound ground turkey
breakfast sausage

1½ cups egg substitute

2 cups lowfat milk

1 teaspoon kosher salt

½ teaspoon coarse
ground black pepper

½ loaf multigrain bread,
torn into chunks

8 ounces sharp cheddar
cheese, shredded

Grease a 9 x 13-inch baking dish and set aside.

Heat oil in a large skillet over medium-high heat. Crumble and brown
the sausage. When cooked through, drain and reserve.

In a large bowl, whisk together the egg substitute, milk, salt, and
pepper. Add sausage, bread, and cheese; stir until evenly coated.
Pour into baking dish, cover with ovenproof lid or aluminum foil, and
refrigerate overnight.

The following day, preheat the oven to 350°F.

Place the covered casserole into the oven and bake for 45 minutes.
Uncover, reduce heat to 325°F, and continue cooking until puffed
and golden brown, another 10 to 15 minutes.

# Brunch: A Discussion

From the look of me, one wouldn't think that I start more days than most at the gym, but I do. What was once a situation so fraught with fear and shame for being the fat kid is now strangely comfortable and even a little bit exhilarating. The treadmill is now my friend and it is definitely keeping me healthier. I even own several pairs of gym shoes and hoard college sweatshirts. Who'da thunk it?

The great reward for all of this, for me and my other half, is a diner breakfast. We like nothing more than going straight from the gym to a greasy spoon and sitting at the counter. There, I chug black iced coffee, preferably served in a chilly metal milkshake can for an added brain freeze. We order egg white omelets and that's how we love to start our days. Now mind you, all of this business is usually over and done with by 8:30am.

So for us, the idea of brunch is breathtakingly irrelevant, if not just plain unpleasant. Even *The New York Times* proclaimed, just as I am writing this rant, that "Brunch Is for Jerks." Don't get me wrong: I LOVE to cook breakfast. I have mastered soft, fluffy scrambled eggs and silky omelets. I leave butter out to soften overnight for perfect toast and I know my way around crispy bacon and beautifully glazed sausages. But anyone who likes champagne in their orange juice at 11:00am is going to be bitterly disappointed. "The kitchen is closed!" my mom used to say around 9, after the last breakfast dish was loaded into the dishwasher. Breakfast? Certainly. Lunch? Absolutely. But there is something so *provincial* about that netherworld of fanned out strawberries and a twisted orange slice cozying up to scrambled eggs close to the noon hour. I guess it's just not my thing.

# EGG WHITE OMELET WITH SMOKED SALMON AND SAUTÉED ONION

*Serves 1*

1 tablespoon canola oil

¼ cup minced onion

3 egg whites

¼ cup chopped smoked salmon

½ teaspoon kosher salt

¼ teaspoon coarse ground black pepper

Spicy Hollandaise (page 166)

Heat oil in a small nonstick skillet over medium-high heat. Add onion and sauté until lightly browned. Add egg whites and stir lightly to distribute. Scatter salmon over eggs. Allow omelet to firm up. As soon as it slides easily in the pan and the edges begin to crisp, flip and fold onto a hot plate. Nap with Spicy Hollandaise.

*continued>*

# SPICY HOLLANDAISE

¼ cup fresh lemon juice

3 egg yolks

1 teaspoon water

1 stick butter, room temperature, divided into quarters

Coarse salt

Coarse ground black pepper

1 tablespoon Sriracha

In a small saucepan over medium-high heat, boil lemon juice until reduced by half. Remove from heat and whisk in egg yolks and water. Continue to whisk on and off the heat until egg yolks thicken to a paste. Once this is accomplished, slowly add the butter and continue whisking on and off the heat, waiting 20 seconds before adding additional butter. Once all butter is incorporated, add salt, pepper, and Sriracha. Keep warm over a slightly larger pot of hot water.

Should the sauce break, simply whisk in an additional egg yolk, again moving the saucepan on and off the heat.

# WOWIE APPLE PANCAKE

*Makes one 12-inch pan*

*Serves 6 to 8*

4 eggs

1 cup milk

1 cup flour

½ teaspoon salt

½ cup (1 stick) unsalted butter

1 large Granny Smith Apple, cored and sliced

½ cup sugar mixed with 1 teaspoon cinnamon

Powdered sugar, for garnish

Maple syrup, warm, for serving

Preheat oven to 450°F.

In a large bowl, whisk together the eggs, milk, flour, and salt. Let rest in the refrigerator for 10 minutes.

*continued>*

Melt butter over medium-high heat in a 12-inch cast-iron or nonstick ovenproof skillet. When the foaming subsides, add apples and half of the sugar mixture. Once apples begin to soften, add batter and the rest of the sugar mixture. Immediately place into the preheated oven and bake until the pancake puffs and browns.

Remove from oven and sprinkle with powdered sugar. Slice and serve with warm maple syrup.

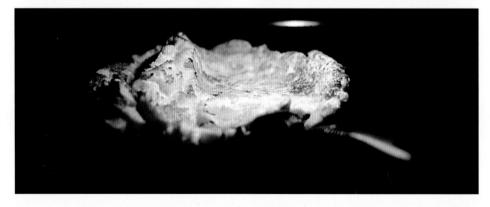

# How to be a good party guest

*"Be pretty if you can, be witty if you must, but be gracious if it kills you."*
—Elsie de Wolfe

Being a good guest is an art form. It requires a delicate balance of personality, curiosity and self-sufficiency.

There is nothing worse than a guest who gives nothing—and I don't mean a hostess gift (more about that on page 115.) I mean a guest who arrives and just sits and doesn't say a word. One year we had a big crowd in for the Super Bowl. There were TVs everywhere, tons of nibbles, and chafing dishes steaming away with chili and other hot dips. But as God is my witness, one couple came in, parked themselves on the sofa, said nothing, and left after the game ended. The entire party swirled around them; honestly, the throw pillows had more personality. I can't even remember their names.

The best guests are the ones who arrive happy and light up the room. They seem genuinely grateful to be in your home and circulate through the crowd greeting friends and introducing themselves to strangers. They are intuitive and can spot a newcomer and draw them in. They don't gather in cliques or take themselves on house tours looking to see what's new. They don't leave with your new Diptyque room spray in their purse.

While we're talking about things that smell nice, whatever you do, *do not show up with flowers*. I have written about it, spoken about it and tweeted ad nauseam. I don't care if it's the first black iris of the season or your mother's prizewinning rose or tulips from the Netherlands—save it for later. What is an awful nuisance the night of a party is a delight the next day, especially with a nice handwritten note.

# GAME DAY GATHERINGS

◆◆◆

Several years ago, my life was turned upside down when I met a handsome, hunky guy from Wisconsin who—don't ask me why—liked me enough to marry me. He's a Michigan grad and, like pretty much everyone in Wisconsin, a rabid sports fan. So here I am, this precious easterner with a penchant for cashmere sweaters and velvet slippers, finding myself smack dab in the middle of Packers land.

Now, my father has always been extremely athletic. Tennis, squash, skiing, sailing, you name it—he has done it and done it well. We were never big on football or baseball, not that my dad didn't try to get me interested in playing or at least watching. But I was hopelessly, well, hopeless.

Fast forward to now and much of my life is spent in suburban bliss in Wauwatosa, a sweet town just over the Milwaukee city line. We live in a rather nondescript 1950s ranch house amongst charming 1920s stone Tudors, truly the ugly duckling in a neighborhood of swans. Rich, my other half, was never a big entertainer. He can cook basic stuff for himself, and, believe me, he loves to eat—although it doesn't show. Well, of course, I had to change all that and turn our house into the Washington Highlands center of gracious living and nonstop entertaining. Jeez, I'm really a piece of work, aren't I?

Being a successful entertainer in Wisconsin means knowing how to host a proper Game Day. You can't call it brunch or lunch or dinner because the timing is totally dependent on kickoff, although the spirit of the menu remains the same regardless of time of day. Don't get me started talking about the duration. I love my new life in the Midwest, but people sure do like to stay . . . and stay. I made the grievous mistake of calling our first cocktail party, in East Coast fashion, from six to eight. At eleven o'clock I was making frozen pizzas. No one had any intention of leaving as long as the booze was holding out.

This same aspect also applies to Game Day. One must be prepared to serve an entire day's worth of small bites, entrées, salads and desserts—over and over and over. Rich says, "Midwesterners like to party." I say, "They clearly have no place else to go." It's a good thing that Midwesterners are also the nicest, most down-to-earth people I've ever met. So this is what I cook for them—and what they seem to enjoy eating.

# WISCONSIN SPREAD

*Serves a few or a crowd*

Sliced summer sausage

Sliced sharp cheddar cheese

Sliced pepper Jack cheese

Garlic dill cheese curds

1 pint Bucky Badger Creamy Horseradish Cheese Spread

1 box original Triscuits

1 jar gherkins, very cold

Place all ingredients on a big wooden board or ceramic platter, serve, and forget about it.

# BLT DIP

*Makes about 4 cups*

1 (4.3-ounce) package bacon bits

8 ounces cream cheese, softened

1 cup sour cream

1 cup mayonnaise

1 cup chopped tomatoes

1 cup chopped scallions, white and green parts

1 teaspoon coarse ground black pepper

Tortilla chips, for serving

Mix all ingredients together and put into a 6-inch ovenproof ramekin.

Bake for 20 minutes at 375°F, or until bubbly and browned.

Serve with tortilla chips.

# SMOKED ALMOND DIP

*Makes 1 1/2 cups*

1 (6-ounce) can smoked almonds

2 cloves fresh garlic

1 bunch parsley, cleaned and stemmed

1 cup plain Greek yogurt

1/4 cup mayonnaise

Pinch of sugar

1 bell pepper, top removed and hollowed out

Raw vegetables for serving

Place almonds and garlic in a food processor fitted with a steel blade; pulse until mixture resembles a coarse meal. Add parsley, yogurt, mayonnaise, and sugar and process until smooth. Transfer to a bowl and refrigerate. Prior to serving, transfer dip into the hollowed-out bell pepper and surround with various sliced raw vegetables.

# SALT LAKE CITY POTATOES

*Serves 10 to 12*

½ cup (1 stick) butter

1 medium onion, diced

2 (10¾-ounce) cans cream of chicken soup

1 pint sour cream

1½ cups shredded cheddar cheese

1 (32-ounce) bag frozen tater tots

2 cups corn flake crumbs

2 tablespoons melted butter

Preheat the oven to 350°F.

In a small sauté pan over medium-high heat, melt ½ cup butter and sauté onions until golden brown. Transfer to a large bowl and combine with soup, sour cream, and cheese.

Scatter tater tots in a lightly buttered 9 x 13-inch baking dish, and pour cheese mixture over the top.

In a small bowl, combine corn flake crumbs with 2 tablespoons melted butter. Sprinkle over potato mixture. Bake for about 30 minutes, until the dish is bubbling and the topping is lightly browned.

# CHILI ELIZABETH TAYLOR

*Serves 8 to 10*

2 tablespoons vegetable oil

1 large Vidalia onion, chopped

2 pounds ground turkey

1/4 cup chili powder

1 tablespoon cumin

1 tablespoon sugar

1 teaspoon cayenne pepper

1 teaspoon kosher salt

1/2 teaspoon coarse
ground black pepper

2 (15.5-ounce) cans kidney
beans, drained and rinsed

1 cup plus 2 tablespoons
water, divided

1 bay leaf

2 tablespoons cornstarch

1 (8.5-ounce) box
corn muffin mix

1/3 cup milk

1 egg

1 (4-ounce) can
chopped jalapeños

1 cup shredded cheddar cheese,
plus additional for serving

1 cup frozen corn

Sour cream, for serving

Chopped green onions,
for garnish

Preheat the oven to 375°F.

In a large sauté pan, heat oil over medium-high heat. Add onions and cook for 1 to 2 minutes, until soft. Add turkey and cook over medium-high heat until browned and cooked through. Stir in chili powder, cumin, sugar, cayenne, salt, pepper, beans, 1 cup water, and bay leaf. Bring to a boil and reduce to a simmer.

In a small bowl, mix cornstarch with 2 tablespoons water to form a slurry. While chili is simmering, slowly pour in cornstarch mixture and mix vigorously until incorporated and mixture has thickened. Pour chili into a large soufflé dish and reserve.

In a large bowl, combine corn muffin mix, milk, egg, jalapeños, 1 cup shredded cheese, and corn. Mix well. Pour on top of the chili. Bake for 20 to 30 minutes, until golden and bubbly.

Serve with sour cream, green onions, and shredded cheese.

# What makes a good party host?

*"Fasten your seatbelts, it's going to be a bumpy night!"*
—Bette Davis as Margo Channing in *All About Eve*

A good party host must be the ultimate facilitator for people to have a good time. It is a totally unselfish undertaking, so those who need to be the center of attention should probably not entertain, as it won't be about them. One needs to be adaptable to any deviation from plan, nuanced to adjust any and every element in real time, and unabashedly fearless.

From the moment the first guest walks through the door until the last candle is blown out, it's a bit of a stage performance. Creativity helps, generosity is essential, but above all, once must have a sense of humor about pretty much everything—from a spilled glass of red wine on a white rug to a burnt roast. It's going to happen at one time or another, so why get all bent out of shape?

A party definitely takes on the personality of the host—their strengths and their weaknesses. Control freaks have the most wretched parties. You can feel the tension in the air if things don't go exactly as planned. These are the ones where you look at your watch after the first drink. But a party given by a relaxed, confident host is a thing of beauty. There's nothing better.

## ACKNOWLEDGMENT TO ALISSA AND STACEY

The first cookbook of any substance that I was aware of was my mom's double-volume set of *The Gourmet Cookbook* that lived on our library shelf next to LPs of operas and Broadway musicals. Leather-bound and imposing, it automatically opened up to the recipe for Sauce Béarnaise, which I still use to this day. The few photographs in the book were frightening, things like Chaud Froid de Poulet, which looked more like an alien from space than an elegant luncheon dish. Even the great Julia Child thought that pictures of her unbaked Pithiviers Jambon et Fromage looked like a "disembodied something."

This is why I am so grateful that the dishes in this book look so darn delectable. I owe that to the extraordinary talents of Alissa Dragun, whose photos truly capture the spirit of the food that I love to cook and serve. Aiding and abetting this effort was my sister, Stacey Stolman, a professionally trained chef, food stylist and recipe developer. Not only did she test and format every recipe for accuracy, she made sure that every fleck of parsley was where it should be as the camera clicked away.

Together, these two talented professionals formed my dream team. Thank you both for helping me bring this book to life!

# *Acknowledgments*

IN APPRECIATION

I had the great fortune to learn so much about living well from some extraordinary women. These ladies were as admired for their exquisite personal style as they were for their cooking, and each one taught me something about gracious hospitality and entertaining that I will carry with me forever. I miss them all more than words can ever say.

Trina Pross

Florence Pushker

Marion Smith

Pauline Trigère

Flo Weinstein

HEARTFELT THANKS TO:

Madge Baird for her editorial wisdom.

Suzanne Taylor, Sheryl Dickert and Melissa Dymock for their design sensibilities and execution.

Gloria and Joseph Stolman for raising me right.

Rich Wilkie for liking pretty much everything I cook and cleaning up after me.

Anyone and everyone who has ever invited me into their own home. If I haven't returned the kindness, I look forward to having you over someday.

# Index

# METRIC CONVERSION CHART

| Volume Measurements | | Weight Measurements | | Temperature Conversion | |
|---|---|---|---|---|---|
| U.S. | Metric | U.S. | Metric | Fahrenheit | Celsius |
| 1 teaspoon | 5 ml | 1/2 ounce | 15 g | 250 | 120 |
| 1 tablespoon | 15 ml | 1 ounce | 30 g | 300 | 150 |
| 1/4 cup | 60 ml | 3 ounces | 90 g | 325 | 160 |
| 1/3 cup | 75 ml | 4 ounces | 115 g | 350 | 180 |
| 1/2 cup | 125 ml | 8 ounces | 225 g | 375 | 190 |
| 2/3 cup | 150 ml | 12 ounces | 350 g | 400 | 200 |
| 3/4 cup | 175 ml | 1 pound | 450 g | 425 | 220 |
| 1 cup | 250 ml | 2 1/4 pounds | 1 kg | 450 | 230 |